BAILOUT

About The Author

Reginald Stuart is a national correspondent for *The New York Times* and chief of its Detroit news bureau. He has been a staff reporter for the newspaper since 1974.

Stuart, a native of Nashville, received his Bachelor of Science degree in Sociology from Tennessee State University and a Master's degree in Journalism from Columbia University.

The author's professional career began in 1968 as a staff reporter for the *Nashville Tennessean.* Afterwards, he spent nearly two years in broadcast journalism as a radio and television news writer and reporter for the WNGE stations of Nashville.

Free lancing has led the author into writing on the reorganization of state systems of higher education in the South with author John Egerton. He also has worked as staff volunteer for the Nashville Branch, NAACP, where he concentrated on improving black presence in the media.

Joining *The New York Times* in March, 1974, he was appointed a business and financial writer and has since focused on economic reporting. Besides general assignment responsibilities, Stuart is chief automotive writer for *The New York Times*, and has won several awards including the Carter G. Woodson Award for Journalism and the Headliners Award for television news team reporting.

Reginald Stuart was the RCA-NBC Journalism Fellow in 1970 at Columbia University.

BAILOUT

The Story Behind America's Billion Dollar Gamble on The 'New' Chrysler Corporation

Reginald Stuart

and books
South Bend, Indiana

338.76292
S93b

BAILOUT. The Story Behind America's Billion Dollar
Gamble on The 'New' Chrysler Corporation.

Copyright © 1980 by Reginald Stuart

ISBN: 0-89708-050-5

First Printing, November 1980

Manufactured in the United States of America

Additional copies available:
the distributors
702 South Michigan
South Bend, IN 46618

To my Mother and late Father
who nurtured my early romance with writing
and my wife, family and friends
who now tolerate it.

Contents

Chapter 1

"...we have no other assumptions that we will make, nor do we feel that any other assumption need be made."
                                                          John J. Riccardo

It was a corporate bailout to which all America had become party, willing or not. The Chrysler Corporation, the 14th largest company in America in 1979, and a key partner in the powerful automobile industry — the nation's largest private employer and consumer of steel, glass and rubber — was on the brink of disaster, only to be saved in the eleventh hour by the American taxpayer. The bailout meant that the United States Government was reluctantly agreeing to repay some 400 nervous Chrysler lenders world wide $1.5 billion in loans to the nearly bankrupt Chrysler should the automaker fail to do so. These loans bought Chrysler valuable time to reorganize, set up a better management team and, hopefully, produce more competitive automobiles.

There was, of course, an outside chance such a gamble to save the 'New' Chrysler Corporation would pay off, thus sparing American taxpayers the agony of covering a bet viewed across the nation as socially sound but fiscally questionable. Yet the odds seemed much greater than the gamble was a losing proposition from the start. Even as early as the summer of 1979, when Chrysler made its first public appeal for government salvation, it was evident that it would lose some $2.5 billion during the 1978-1980 period. These losses were unparalleled in the history of corporate America, and with that in mind, many opponents of the proposed bailout cried that any funding would simply be good money thrown after bad. Any government backed loans to Chrysler, they reasoned, would only delay the inevitable — a Chrysler bankruptcy.

That such a proposal was ever made and seriously considered, was, in itself, more significant than the odds placed on the outcome of the Chrysler bailout. Liberals and conservatives alike were unsettled with the idea that the American government, for the first time, would become a full public partner in an American private enterprise of such magnitude. Further, the bailout was bound to have implications beyond American shores. Still, with all the obvious complications, the government agreed to the bailout, perhaps mostly from fear of the unknown. It strongly feared the possible consequences of allowing such a major industrial force as Chrysler to collapse especially in 1980, a presidential election year and during what was rapidly growing into an economic slide, the likes of which this nation had not seen since the Great Depression.

As events unfolded — from that summer afternoon in July, when John J. Riccardo, then chairman and chief executive officer of Chrysler, announced at Chrysler headquarters in Highland Park that he was formally asking the Federal government to save the failing company, until the actual signing of the loan guarantee documents nearly a year later — a more frightening reality was rapidly coming to fore. The entire American automobile industry, which in just three generations had grown into a bastion of industrial strength envied worldwide, suddenly was in deep trouble. America's competitive edge in the world marketplace was sliding, vehicle sales were in an avalanche, hundreds of thousands of workers were thrown out of work; the automobile economy had ground to a halt and corporate losses were running at record levels.

The automobile industry was faltering under converging pressures it had been immune to or unfamiliar with during its decades of growth prior to World War II and the successful decade immediately following. The new list was long and potent, including tough government regulations covering traffic safety, automobile pollution and fuel efficiency; steady and challenging competition from long-ignored foreign automobile manufacturers; traumatic sales slumps in the 1970's precipitated by abrupt gasoline shortages, followed by skyrocketing gasoline prices, and finally, the cash shortages brought on by quantum leaps in new product spending required by the government and the foreign competition.

Detroit's troubles were not solely the product of external developments. Aware for years, through their business activities in Europe and the Orient, of rising fuel prices and therefore the need for fuel-efficient automobiles, American automakers merely toyed with the idea of making such vehicles for American consumers. There was never any fear that the land of milk and honey, with large cars loaded with luxury items and run by high-powered engines fueled by cheap gasoline, would suddenly find its tanks empty and refillable only at unbelieveably higher prices. When faced with such a prospect in the mid-1970's, the automobile industry made some token gestures toward retreating from the days of excess. But it tried even harder to ignore the shocking realities of American mobility being controlled by foreign nations whose agendas might not be compatible with that of America. So when the industry crash of 1979 arrived, Detroit found itself far from ready in ideas and short of strategies, not to mention new products.

The Chrysler Corporation, poorly managed during

many of its 55 years, was not alone this time. Its major competitors — the smaller American Motors Corporation, and the much larger Ford Motor Company and General Motors Corporation — were ailing almost as badly. For the first time in history, all of the automakers faced ending a year, 1980, with substantial losses, each in dire need of loans from outside sources to finance their new product efforts and in near panic over whether their new small-car era products would sell well enough to turn their fortunes around.

Thus the writing of a new and crucial chapter in American history began when, in June, 1980, the United States Chrysler Loan Guarantee Board, acting under the authority of the Chrysler Loan Guarantee Act of 1979, gave a gasping Chrysler Corporation the legislative revival it needed: the right to borrow funds with repayment guaranteed by the government. The loan guarantee was preceded by political and economic pressures from many sectors of society and massive financial concessions by labor, as well as policy-making concessions by Chrysler management, all unprecedented. Yet the funds were on their way, and like a crowd gathered around a Las Vegas gambling casino table to witness a high-stakes game of the night, labor, government and business leaders worldwide took special note of the Chrysler rescue action. The fascination was not so much with the bailout's eventual outcome, but rather its historic precedents and implications for the future of America. With the stroke of a pen, Chrysler, founded in 1925 and one of America's 20 largest companies during most of the 1970's, removed itself from the ranks of private enterprise and became a government-sponsored corporation. By the same action, the United States Government made an unprecedented leap into one of the holiest domains of private enterprise — the American automobile industry. Both may have taken steps that would eventually prove irreversible.

Against those developments, the Chrysler bailout was emerging as more than just a risky effort to salvage the thousands of jobs of Chrysler workers across the nation and jobs in related industries, as well as the financial health of those large and small lenders who had loaned Chrysler a total of $4.4 billion. The bailout had become the blueprint by which help from all segments of society might be solicited for any ailing American industry if America was to hold its ground as an industrial power with which to be reckoned.

Chapter 2

At the turn of the century the great American railroads, nurtured by the generosity of the government, dominated American transportation. Having displaced the stagecoach companies and inland and coastal ship lines, the railroads became the most advanced modes of transportation, numbering over 600 separate companies. The rails carried millions of people daily to and from nearly every big and small town with whistle-stops in between. Where rails left off, horse drawn carriages took up their traditional function. But another mode of transportation was on the horizon that would silence the horse-drawn carriages and later threaten the railroads with extinction.

In 1900 there were 8,000 privately owned passenger cars on the roads. Outside a handful of big cities, they were rare and frightening oddities; they popped, smoked, jerked and moved at outlandish speeds of 10 to 20 miles per hour. But by 1979 there were 120 million privately owned passenger cars on the road; nearly 85 percent of all United States households owned one or automobiles.

When trucks, more rare than cars in 1900, were added, the number of vehicles in 1979 exceeded 150 million. Considered by all as luxury items in the early days, automobiles quickly became necessities as the nation's populace and its work force spread from the central cities. The spread helped fuel the growth of the auto industry and, in turn, the industry helped fuel the spreading. Another dimension, not to be overlooked, was the fascination that the automobile commanded as an important status and sex symbol. Back seats became instant bedrooms and the size of one's machine reflected the size of one's ego, if not one's financial abilities.

As an institution, the automobile revolutionized transportation just as the telephone did personal communications. The resulting decline in mass transportation was equally startling. It was not until the late 1970's that the once-gigantic railroad industry, which gave up after World War II on transporting people and shifted its emphasis to freight and other ventures, would even have the opportunity to make a possible comeback — as an alternative to suddenly high-cost fuel and cars.

America was nearly a full generation behind Europe in the development of the automobile. As early as the late 1860's, Siegfried Marcus, a German, began experiments in Vienna with carriages powered by gasoline combustion engines. After several years of unsuccessfully trying to interest private investors and government authorities in the potential of his experiments, Marcus abandoned his projects and donated his materials to a museum. Several years later, in 1876, Nikolaus Otto, another German engineer, received a patent on an engine that was also based on internal combustion — an expulsion of energy caused by mixing air with gasoline in specific portions. (In 1879, George Selden, one of the first to toy with automobiles in America did apply for a patent on his internal combustion power carriage. But it was not granted until 1895 and Selden never built his car. By the time the idea of building horseless-powered carriages had caught on in America, his ideas were considered outdated. In an attempt to protect his patents, Selden lost a celebrated case to Henry Ford, thus opening the door to many who wanted to enter the auto-making sweepstakes.)

In the mid 1880's, Gottlieb Daimler and Karl Benz, again both Germans, but working independently, adapted the Otto-type engine successfully into small carriages. The internal combustion engine was rapidly emerging as a contender with the popular steam engine and electric battery motor as a preferable power source, as what is now known as the automobile began to gain public acceptance. In France, Armand Peugeot and Emile Levassor, working together with Benz engines, became the world's leading automobile maker by the early 1890's. At the same time, the roots of an industrial revolution had been firmly planted in America and to some aspiring entrepreneurs, the automobile seemed the logical step after railroads. On September 21, 1893, Charles and Frank Duryea, two young bicycle mechanics in Springfield, Massachusetts, rolled out a vehicle based on Benz's internal-combustion engine, sounding the gun that started the auto race. With more information on the Benz technology available, others added their personal touches and new vehicles began to blossom.

By 1900, conservative estimates were that 72 American companies, including carriage makers, bicycle makers, wagon manufacturers, people who tinkered with machinery as a hobby and even a plumber named David Buick, all were making versions of the automobile. The number of companies mushroomed into the hundreds before several shakeouts, starting just before World War I and ending in the late 1930's after the Great Depression, cut it back to just nine.

From the onset of American development of the automobile, there were considerable differences of opinion over the preferable source of power. Despite interest in the internal combustion engine, just as much time and money was on steam powered, as well as electric-powered vehicles. But the more the latter two were tried, the more attractive the internal-combustion engine became. engine became.

Unlike the electric vehicle, the internal combustion engine did not require constant battery recharging. With improvements on the self-starter, the electric vehicle lost another advantage. The steam-powered engine was handicapped by its long start-up time, high cost and complexity. Eventually numerous promising ventures fell victim to their own unwillingness or inability to adapt to the internal combustion engine, among them the popular Stanley Steamer.

For a brief time a battle of sorts appeared likely between the Northeast and Middle West over which region would emerge as the hub of the industry. The question was resolved for all practical purposes by 1910 in favor of the Middle West. Western Pennsylvania, Ohio and Indiana were rich in petroleum resources, the fuel needed to power the internal combustion engine. But Detroit, a leading carriage producer for roads and rails and a major shipbuilding city, had the edge in human resources — and money. The city's location on the Great Lakes had encouraged shipbuilding and the vast timber resources of Southeastern Michigan attracted carriage builders to the area. By 1910, the shipworks had spawned the largest assemblage of skilled engineers in the nation while the carriage business commanded a huge corps of veteran craftsmen. The fortunes generated by these industries bankrolled such pioneers as Ford, Cadillac, Buick, Olds and Packard.

During the formative years of the automobile business, many would-be industry czars went out of the business even before they got a running start. Policy differences, money problems and personality conflicts ruined many an idea of great potential. Ransom Olds left Oldsmobile only months after the first car was produced because he and his lumber industry backers could not agree on the type of car the company should try to make and sell. William Durant, the man who created the General Motors Corporation, almost ran it into the ground twice by overextending the company. After a first venture failed, Henry Ford walked out on his partners. Likewise, in his second venture he left after refusing to allow the installation of major components of another manufacturer in his automobiles. More fortunate than many others, Ford rebounded with new backers.

Still many survived, thanks largely to the concentration of shipbuilding, lumber and railroad wealth in that city. When a semi-attractive automobile venture was said to be on the skids, a group of investors always appeared to be waiting in the wings to pick up where a prior group had failed. Had that not been the case, two of the best known names of the automobile business today — Ford Motor and General Motors — would probably not exist.

By 1980, however, the competitive mood in America was considerably different. The modern day auto industry leaders, hungry for help as their predecessors had been in the formative years, learned that American private enterprise has lost much of the entrepreneurial spirit which has made the nation envied around the world. There were no eager takers among the well-heeled and financially influential. The changing nature of the high stakes game of automobile manufacturing and marketing and the fact that Americans no longer controlled the tables had dampened much of the enthusiasm that in earlier years might have arisen.

An early name to surface from the pool of early manufacturers was William Crapo Durant. Durant was the grandson of Henry Crapo, a Flint, Michigan, lumber magnate who had parlayed his fortune and influence into election as governor of the State of Michigan. An assembler of business ventures rather than a skilled manufacturer, Durant and his friend Dallas Dort borrowed the funds to purchase a small carriage company for

$2,000. They hired the skilled help necessary to build small carts to be sold for $25 each. By the turn of the century, the ambitious 40-year-old had turned Durant-Dort Carriage Company into the largest carriage and wagon maker in America and had earned millions.

Also in Flint, Michigan, at the time, was a struggling company operated by David Buick, a plumber who hoped to strike it rich in the new auto industry. The demands of the business were more than Buick and his financial backers could sustain. After selling only 16 cars in 1903 and 37 the following year, they persuaded Durant, as an astute business tycoon, to take over the company. Durant, one of the pioneer super salesmen of the industry, capitalized his new automobile company with $1.5 million in stock and personally solicited sales. That same year, Ransom Olds, whose Oldsmobiles had sold 6,500 units in 1904, fell out with his lumber-money backers. Oldsmobile had become the largest volume automobile manufacturer in the world, yet the backers felt that the company could do best by focusing on the luxury market. Olds, on the other hand, had wanted the company to concentrate its efforts upon more affordable models. Unable to resolve their differences, Olds left the company.

By 1908, Durant had not only revived Buick but also had turned it into the biggest seller of cars, with 8,487 units and a handsome profit of $1.7 million. In that same year, Durant bought Oldsmobile for $3 million in stock and incorporated the two into the General Motors Company. Durant quickly became obsessed with growth. In this new industry, he wanted to duplicate what he had accomplished in the carriage business. In two brief years, between 1908 and 1910, General Motors acquired controlling interest in some 20 automobile companies. The most significant of the group was the Cadillac Motor Company, for which General Motors paid $4.5 million.

Economic disaster struck General Motors in 1910 when, severely overextended, it was unable to pay its bills and was forced to shut down many of its operations. Making matters worse, Henry Ford had introduced his Ford Model-T in 1908 and with it claimed first place in the industry. Ford remained in the lead for the next 17 years until 1927. As part of a five-year reorganization plan, Durant was forced from the presidency of his company by James J. Storrow, chairman of General Motors' finance committee and the head of a Boston investment banking house, Lee Higginson & Company. Several years later, Charles Nash, the works manager at Buick who was named president of General Motors in 1912, played a major role in nursing the company back to health.

Durant, still a major stockholder in General Motors in 1911, used his own resources and those of new backers to begin the production of yet another automobile — the Chevrolet. The new car was based on the concepts of Louis Chevrolet, a prominent race car driver. Chevrolet had worked at Buick during Durant's reign over General Motors and had set the basics of another car Durant was then making, called the "Little Car." The Chevrolet became a financial jewel. Durant used Chevrolet's profits on his favorite pastime, playing the stock market, where he quietly bought up more General Motors stock. By the autumn of 1915, Durant surprised his former associates with the news that they no longer controlled the company — he did. Since no one had a majority with which to determine the company's policy Durant reached a compromise with Pierre S. DuPont. The chemical magnate was a director of General Motors and named three directors to the board. At the November 16, 1915 board meeting, DuPont was elected chairman. Within several months Durant, like a champ on the rebound, regained his lost crown, first as a director and then, when Nash resigned on June 1, 1916, as president.

Durant remained in control of Chevrolet as well, which in a short time had grown to be a major competitor of General Motors. By 1917, Durant had built Chevrolet's holdings to 450,000 out of 825,000 shares, more than half of the outstanding General Motors stock. In the following year Durant gained full control of both companies and merged Chevrolet into General Motors. In addition, Buick, the automobile company that Durant had salvaged in 1904 and turned into a money machine by 1908, had been returned to its admirable position in the sales and profits department under the hands of Walter P. Chrysler, a relative newcomer to the industry. Durant, however, used the Buick profits liberally in his resumption of empire building. In another acquisition, costing $13.5 million in cash and stock, Durant purchased the Hyatt Roller Bearing Company of Newark, New Jersey. It was headed by Alfred P. Sloan Jr., an electrical engineering graduate from the Massachusetts Institute of Technology, who later became the driving force behind the industrial giant known today as General Motors.

By 1920 Durant had almost run his empire into the ground for a second time. Tough competition from Ford with his Model-T, the post World War I economic slide, and too much free-wheeling with General Motors resources by Durant and his officers had put the company in far deeper debt than first realized. Walter P. Chrysler, one of the officers who protested to Durant about his activities, left General Motors in disgust to emerge a few years later as the head of his own company. Durant, who continued to play on the stock market to build his personal fortune, had accumulated about $14 million in personal debts that he could not cover. He had used his General Motors stock as security, the same stock that at one time was considered as valuable as gold. As the Hunt Brothers of Texas were to find with silver in 1980, stock certificates lose value also.

Durant turned to Pierre DuPont for help. In 1916,

DuPont, his company basking in the wealth it had accumulated from selling munitions to both sides during World War I, purchased 26.4 percent of General Motors from Durant for $43 million. With the understanding that Durant would sever his management ties with General Motors once and for all, DuPont arranged to bailout General Motors (and in turn DuPont itself). A new stock issue of 3.2 million shares at a price of $20 per share was set. Explosives Trades Limited of Great Britain purchased 1.8 million of these shares, while J.P. Morgan, the banking house of New York City, purchased the rest. DuPont took over as president of General Motors, vesting all operating responsibilities in the hands of Alfred Sloan Jr., who was named its president in May, 1923. Sloan later became chairman in May, 1937, a position he held until his retirement in April of 1956.

Sloan quickly reorganized General Motors, discarding the Durant style of free-wheeling conglomerateur. In its place, Sloan introduced DuPont's method of decision by committee, a management approach that has since been copied by many other corporations. It provided for greater fiscal control over the company from a central headquarters. Sloan also created a management system which constantly groomed people to succeed each other, so that, regardless of the task, plant manager or company chairman, there would always be two or three people capable of assuming new duties within hours. In the opinion of some at General Motors, the committee system had its flaws, but most recognized that it was better than the management styles of the competition, an opinion that still holds true.

By 1927, through advanced styling and engineering, as well as decisions to stimulate sales by making frequent model changes which outdated every new product sold, General Motors successfully replaced Ford Motor Company as the leading manufacturer of automobiles in America; a position it would never lose again. Ford, meanwhile, saw its sales drop by 50 percent as a result of Henry

Ford's forced decision to discontinue production of the Model-T after some 18 impressive years on the market. Starting in late May of 1927, Henry Ford closed his Dearborn plant for six months and converted his entire production network to the Model-A. It was a belated but necessary move which cost Ford Motor Company dearly.

Under the increasing competitive pressures in the 1920's posed by General Motors and Ford, taps were played for numerous smaller competitors, including Haynes, Franklin, Peerless, Stutz, Apperson and Rickenbacker, and Paige. Durant, whose final departure from General Motors included $3 million in General Motors stock, continued his automobile manufacturing and organized Durant Motors, which lasted until 1930. In 1936, Durant filed for bankruptcy, listing his debts of $914,000 and his assets of $250.

Then came the Great Depression. General Motors' hold on the automobile marketplace solidified as even more of its smaller competitors fell by the wayside. In three-years time, between 1929 and 1932, General Motors' market share rose from 32 percent to 42 percent, while the independent's share fell to 10 percent from 25 percent. Ford Motor Company and the Chrysler Corporation split the other 48 percent.

General Motors was fast on the way to fulfilling its corporate goal of producing a "product for every purse and purpose" and fulfilling the Durant dream of building an economic and political empire second to none.

The jewel that had always eluded Durant through the years, despite his frequent overtures, was the Ford Motor Company. The distance between these two industrial giants may have been just as well, since both Durant and Ford were men whose visions of the potential of the automobile were only rivaled by their super egos.

Henry Ford, a self-taught engineer, developed his fascination for machines as a teenager while working on his father's farm in Dearborn, Michigan. After graduating from high school in 1879 and completing that fall's harvest, Henry left for the machine shops of Detoit. There he immersed himself in his first love — mechanics. Ford worked on various jobs at several different shops, including one at the Detroit Drydock Company where he was exposed to the internal combustion engine. He returned briefly to farming, but soon heard of an opening for an engineer at the Edison Illuminating Company and, banking on his practical experience and reputation, applied for and got the job. Within two years, Ford became chief engineer at Edison. It was not until December, 1883, however, that he caught the bug and began feverishly trying to develop his own automobile.

Aside from the moral support he received from Charles B. King, a Detroit engineer who also was trying to build an car powered by an internal combustion engine, Ford received little encouragement and much ridicule for his early efforts. But in 1886, young Ford received a needed spark which possibly was the decisive encounter in his life. Thomas Alva Edison, the famed inventor, was attending a meeting of the Association of Edison Illuminating Companies. In the course of a conversation with Edison, Ford's boss casually mentioned that he had an employee who was wasting his time tinkering with internal combustion engines and trying to make an automobile. To everyone's amazement, Edison wanted to hear more and talked enthusiastically with Ford, a gesture the automaker never forgot. Years later, when Ford became wealthy, he built several monuments dedicated to the memory of Edison. Among the most notable are the Greenfield Village and the Henry Ford Museum. Meanwhile, Ford's early supporter, Charles King, sought the blessings of local investors, but had little success because they rejected his ideas as hopeless. Shortly afterwards, King joined the Navy, leaving Ford behind to pursue his efforts quite alone.

Henry Ford's first big break came in 1896 when

William Maybury was elected the mayor of Detroit. Maybury had known Ford for several years and, intrigued by Ford's pursuit of a viable automobile, he granted Ford a special permit to drive experimental cars on the streets of the city. In 1893 Maybury, then an attorney, had unsuccessfully pushed Ford's appointment as the superintendent of Detroit's new municipal power plant. Perhaps as significant, Maybury and three other Detroiters put up $500 each to back Ford.

By July, 1899, Ford had vastly improved his early automobile and received added financial backing. William Murphy, the son of a lumberman and principle stockholder in the Edison Company, joined a host of Detroiters in assembling $15,000 to incorporate the Detroit Automobile Company. Ford was able to quit his work at Edison and devote his full energies to his dream of building automobiles. However, within two years some backers grew anxious over the slowness of developments. In 1901, the company was reorganized with new backers as the Henry Ford Motor Company. The small, new company suffered the same symptoms as the first and soon the venture began to sour and head toward a fruitless end. Henry Ford had great ideas and worked hard at them, but he did so at his own pace. Lacking formal technical training, he was not adept at putting his ideas on paper and, worse, he showed little skill at running a business. To help, Murphy recruited Henry M. Leland, an engineer who had gained an impeccable reputation for his automotive work. Leland was to supply the engines, transmissions and steering mechanisms for a commercial Ford car whose debut was imminent. But instead of showing gratitude, Ford was outraged with the idea, despite the fact that his own production plans were running far behind schedule. Ford insisted that his car would be his car. He left the company in March, 1902.

Leland's power plant, which had initially been intended for use by Oldsmobile before Ransom Olds left the company in disgust with his backers, made it to the market as the Cadillac. Later, Leland made another car of distinction — the Lincoln.

Meanwhile, Henry Ford, despite one business disaster and his withdrawal from another, convinced Alexander Malcomson, a coal yard operator, to finance his efforts. They formed to what soon became the Ford Motor Company, sorely undercapitalized but eager to move ahead, in February, 1903. Ford ordered 650 chassis from the Dodge Brothers, a family that had a strong reputation for making quality automotive components at its machine shop. However, in less than a month, Ford and his new partner were unable to meet their payments to the Dodge Brothers and Malcomson turned to an uncle, John Gray, for economic support. Gray, who became the first president of the Ford Motor Company, agreed to bailout the company by advancing $10,000 in exchange for 105 shares of stock. He also insisted that Ford install James Couzens, Malcomson's office manager, as its business manager. On June 16, 1903, the Ford Motor Company was incorporated with 13 stockholders. Couzens is singularly credited with much of the success of this version of Ford Motor. He was able to keep Henry Ford's mind away from race cars long enough to get the real commercial cars off the drawing board.

In an action similar to the events at Olds, Henry Ford began to differ with Malcomson over product. Ford believed that the company should concentrate on making and selling moderately priced automobiles that would attract the growing middle class. In contrast, Malcomson felt the company would do better shooting for the luxury market since it was a given that automobile transportation was for the enjoyment of the elite. Malcomson went off on his own, setting up a company called Aerocar and financing it with the dividends from his 25-percent holding in Ford Motor. Ford, irritated, and his supporters (Couzens was one), countered by setting up a Ford subsidiary which did two things — lessened Ford Motor's dependence on the Dodge brothers' engines and components and cut into Malcomson's dividends.

Ford won. In 1906, the warring partners decided to part ways. Henry Ford, never credited with having a keen sense for business, wound up in full control of his company, having forced Malcomson to sell out. Aerocar went into bankruptcy in 1907.

With Couzens to help him on the financial side, Ford recruited Walter Flanders, an engineer the caliber of Leland to handle production. To flesh out ideas on paper, he recruited C.H. Wells and Joseph Galamb, two capable engineers. In the autumn of 1908, the first Model-T rolled off the Ford assembly line. It remained in production from 1908 to 1926 with hardly a style change and sold over 15 million units. This successful car also established the Ford Motor Company as an institution in the world industrial community and placed Henry Ford among the most influential, controversial and financially powerful individuals in the nation.

The man whose career appeared destined to be in the electric power industry had found his niche. Although he would lose considerable ground in later years to General Motors by virtue of its more aggressive marketing approaches, the Ford Motor Company would reign for decades as a major industrial force in America as well as the entire world. The next time Ford Motor rubbed shoulders with disaster was in the 1940's, when its creator again almost became its destroyer. Henry Ford, the innovative, controversial iron ruler of Ford Motor, fell victim to age and senility and became prey to unscrupulous aides who surrounded him. Bankruptcy would have certainly met the company in the aftermath of its brilliant role in arming the Allied Forces during World War II, had it not been for a family feud that ended in September, 1945, with Henry Ford relinquishing control of the company to Henry Ford II, his grandson. Young Henry Ford was never able to restore the company to its position of leadership with respect to General Motors since irreversible damage had long since been done. Still, he was able to restore financial health to the company. His also would be a one-man rule until his retirement in 1979 when again many doubts were renewed about its future.

Had the automobile been conceived in the nation's capitol, it probably would have been called the pork barrel, an item specially designed to satisfy the greed of individual regions represented in Congress in order to assure passage of laws. It was probably coincidence, but so diverse were the requirements for creating a single vehicle — lumber, steel, iron, rubber, glass, oil, gas, and the human resources to make, mold and deliver them — that it might as well have been the effort of a clique of members of Congress. As a result, there was general recognition in the business and political community of the broad role a developed automobile industry could play in this century by providing work for the multitudes and riches for the few.

Without even trying, the auto pioneers backed by lumber and railroad monies, had cultivated a Who's Who among the American power brokers. This list included John D. Rockefeller, the oil baron whose profuse wealth became multiplied by his ability to take petroleum 'waste' and convert it into gasoline; J.P. Morgan, the legendary investment banker who assembled the financial packaging for many automobile ventures and foiled others; and Pierre S. DuPont, the chemical magnate, whose personal and corporate fortunes were enriched through the sale of new products for the automobile, but more importantly by his ownership of a controlling interest in the General Motors Corporation for nearly two generations. The alliances that emerged from the mutual interests of these independently powerful forces eventually resulted in immeasurable profits for their coffers and great influence upon the American society and its public and private policy abroad.

Despite its constant growing pangs, by 1925 the American automobile industry had claimed a permanent place in world history. Its achievements outshined and overshadowed its many shortcomings. Most importantly, the industry was guaranteed a role in the shaping of the future of America as long as the nation sought to be an industrial power among nations. Everything seemed so well defined by then that few bothered to think otherwise.

In part because of improvements in the assembly line production at Oldsmobile, America was, by 1906, producing more cars than France. Thus it became the leading producer nation of automobiles. Under the leadership of Henry Leland, creator of the Cadillac, and a handful of other perfectionists, standardization and interchangeability of vehicle parts was achieved, a feat that allowed for mass production at a far lower cost. By 1910, with the success of the Ford Model-T, America was producing more cars than the rest of the world combined.

In addition to producing automobiles, the pioneers realized their potential for political strength by forming the Lincoln Highway Association. With such prominent names as Leland, Roy Chapin and Henry Joy atop the association's letterheads, the group sought to promote the building of the nation's first coast-to-coast highway, and succeeded. The group initially set out to raise $10 million from within the industry to use as matching money with localities. The industry was to supply the plans and materials for a road, while the localities served by the highway were to furnish the machinery and labor. Within a month the idea was endorsed by the National Conference of Governors, despite the fact that there were fewer than three million cars on the road at the time. In 1916, in the first matching grant program established in the nation, Congress adopted the Federal Aid Road act.

Citing the Federal Government's responsiblity under the Constitution to deliver the mail, Congress blessed the automobile industry with a $75 million appropriation to be spent over five years for the construction of Post Roads, that is, roads upon which the mail is delivered. The idea of government sponsorship was similar to the granting of millions of acres of valuable land in the form of rights of way to the railroads in the 1800's that led to the growth of public mass transit. In a similar manner, the government viewed the paving of roadways in the 1900's as embracing the growth of personal transportation. The Lincoln Highway, commonly known as Highway 30, stretching from Atlantic City to San Francisco/Oakland, was completed in the early 1930's when the association was dissolved. In the meantime, numerous highway groups had surfaced to expand upon and pursue the goals of the Lincoln association. Among these was the powerful American Road Builders Association. The Post road law was a sweet first encounter in Washington for the automakers, and in subsequent years it was matched and surpassed by even greater feats.

World War I signaled yet another milestone for the industry. Trucks, far fewer in number and farther back in development than passenger cars, were suddenly being bought for use as battlefield tools of war. By the end of the war, the government had snapped up hundreds of thousands of them, many for resale to foreign nations. At the same time, industry executives were becoming highly visible consultants to the government on how to best mobilize materials and soldiers to fight wars. Roy Chapin, the former General Motors official who had persuaded wealthy Detroit department store owner J. L. Hudson to back Chapin's bid to start an automobile company, served during the war as head of the Highway Transport Committee of the Council for National Defense. Suddenly and convincingly, the automobile industry had established its products and its leaders as essential to our nation's military defense capability. From that point on, the strength of one hinged significantly upon the strength of the other during peace and war.

Following World War I came another round of

shakeouts in the industry during the early and mid-1920's as competition stiffened along with the price of doing business. By the end of the decade the nation experienced the great stock market crash of 1929, a major prelude to the Great Depression. Both were strongly felt in Detroit for sure, but in at least one respect in a quite ironic manner. In October of 1929, the same month of the great stock market crash, Henry Ford had assembled great names from all over the world at the Henry Ford Museum and Greenfield Village. The museum was an enormous indoor showcase of artifacts of American industrial growth, and the village, was a sprawling outdoor museum consisting of the homes, laboratories and workshops of some of the nation's great inventors and educators. The occasion was to honor the 50th anniversary of Thomas Alva Edison's invention of the incandescent bulb. Among the participating guests was the 82-year-old Edison, who 30 years earlier had given Ford encouragement. Also in attendance were J.P. Morgan, President and Mrs. Herbert Hoover, Madame Curie, Albert Einstein, and Orville Wright. Although nominally a tribute to Edison, the event was as much a tribute to the respect which the automobile industry had gained and the clout Ford had amassed in the process.

The Great Depression took its toll on the industry's ranks, as competition toughened amid nosediving sales in the marketplace. Like flies hit by Raid they fell — Durant Motors, Moon Motor Company, Gardner, Elcar, Stearns Knight and Peerless, Jordan, Kissel, Franklin and Nordyke-Marmon. In 1935 Auburn Motors folded, along with R.E.O., which had been organized by Ransom Olds after his departure from Oldsmobile in 1903. Packard survived the great fall, establishing itself as a top-of-the-line carmaker; it remained as the only independent maker in that class of cars.

The 1930's also gave birth to the labor movement throughout the factories of the automobile industry and catapulted the United Automobile Workers union into a position of bargaining-table clout with management and strength on the political front through the ballot box. Professional groups and skilled craft guilds had organized in an effort to protect their jobs from newcomers. Unskilled factory workers, whose earnings were minimal when compared to the profits they helped their employers accumulate and whose lives were plagued by management's denial of acceptable grievance-redress procedures, quickly saw organization as the key to solving many of their problems. After averting a near bloodbath in the winter of 1937 at the General Motors Chevrolet plant in Flint, the industry giant officially recognized the United Auto Workers as the collective bargaining agent for all blue collar workers who chose to have it as their representative. In April 1937, the Chrysler Corporation filed a suit in protest of the General Motors agreement, but soon dropped the action and recognized the union. A confrontation between Ford Motor union busters and union organizers took place on a rail overpass near the huge Rouge plant in Dearborn. After this bloody Battle of the Overpass in Detroit, Henry Ford relented and, under duress, agreed to the United Auto Workers representation of Ford Motor factory workers. In the union, the factory worker saw a chance to prosper in good times and bad.

As the automobile industry grew in size and popularity, management and labor maintained their adversarial postures, with the union occasionally threatening an automaker with irreversible damage by refusing to produce while allowing competitors to run full blast. Although both had common interests, one could not expect them to be on the same side of an issue.

World War II again interrupted America's steadily growing love affair with the automobile. But it provided the industry an unusual opportunity to help the government flex its muscles as never before in history. The industry asserted its existence as a self-contained industrial power, impressed the world, and in the process increased its influence in the nation's capitol. As America entered the war, it was totally self-sufficient with respect to its petroleum needs.

The Japanese bombing of Pearl Harbor on December 7, 1941, and the military developments that drew America into the war caught the nation by surprise, although the likelihood of some American involvement had been growing for some time. Less than a year after the bombing, at the Ford Motor Company Rouge complex, partly constructed with war money, the assembly lines were rolling off a vehicle which became an institution of war — the Jeep. By June 1943, some 1,000 automobile plants across the nation were performing many of the tasks being directed from Detroit and Washington though the tireless work of some 1,250,000 people.

Soon another project was being conducted with much less fanfare — the government's top secret effort to perfect an atomic bomb, commonly referred to as the Manhattan Project. Chrysler had been selected by the government to supply the needed materials and equipment for the huge gaseous diffusion plant at Oak Ridge, Tennessee. Chrysler's significant involvement in the Manhattan Project came when it helped to solve the government's problem of how to build a number of diffusers without tying up the entire production of nickel in the United States and Canada for two years. Nickel was found to be the only metal which would sustain the corrosive effects of the lethal gas — uranium hexaflouride — which was needed to make the atomic bomb effective. Chrysler workers, along with the workers of the Wolverine Tube Company, demonstrated that nickel-plated rather than pure nickel-steel diffusers would achieve the objectives and soon shipped more than 1,000 freight carloads of the diffusion apparatus to Oak Ridge. On August 6, 1945, an American aircraft dropped the atomic bomb upon Hiroshima, Japan, devastating much of the area and killing and maiming thousands. The war was over. Detroit became known

worldwide as the Arsenal of Democracy in recognition
of its war-time performance. It brought America to its
finest hour, many leaders asserted, establishing the nation
as the world's premier industrial power. It brought the
industry more than $22 billion in revenue.

During the next two decades, the automobile industry
supplied the nation with numerous key policy makers,
including two Secretaries of Defense — Charles E. Wilson
of General Motors under Eisenhower and Robert S.
McNamara of Ford Motor in the Johnson administration
— plus a Secretary of Housing and Urban Development,
former American Motors chief, George Romney.

The end of the war was actually the beginning of
a new era of growth for the automobile industry. Despite
the nation's affection for the broad array of well-styled
and significantly improved vehicles, the demand had
been pent up for nearly two decades as a result of the
Great Depression of the 1930's and the war during much
of the 1940's. At the end of the war, less than half the
nation's households owned automobiles, while in less
than ten years, by the end of the 1950's, private
automobile ownership rose to better than 80 percent.
Soldiers, home from the war, had money saved up and
it was burning their pockets. The millions who found
work in the war machine plants had saved up funds
and also were anxious to spend. In the years immediately
following World War II, Detroit found the demand for
its products far outstripped its ability to supply them.
Later it would recognize the decade of the 1950's as a
vintage era when America really got hooked on the
automobile. In response to that demand, Detroit made
bigger and more powerful automobiles. These powerful
cars were a clear reflection of America's muscle.

To facilitate the growing automobile population, the
government stepped in again to aid the industry. In
1956, Congress enacted the Federal Highway Act,
authorizing completion of interstate and defense highways.
The new automobile — a pork barrel project to help

speed riders to their destinations — was planned. By the end of the 1970's, the plans had resulted in the construction of 42,500 miles of interstate highways at a total cost of $60 billion.

Meanwhile, Packard Motors, which had seen its luxury car business decline and its bid to stay in business through a combination of continued government contracts and new offerings of lower-priced cars fail, merged with Studebaker in 1956, signaling the beginning of the final chapter for small independents. They would all eventually merge into what is now American Motors. Also, a small imported car, known as the Volkswagen, appeared on American roads, only to be laughed at by prospering Detroit.

Chapter 3

"There is in manufacturing a creative joy that only poets are supposed to know. Some day I'd like to show a poet how it feels to design and build a railroad locomotive."

Walter P. Chrysler

An amusing thought of 1950 was that a foreign car could possibly pose a challenge to American automobile manufacturers on their own turf. Likewise, only 25 years earlier a similarly outlandish idea would have been for a new automobile company to be formed which could rattle the cages of Ford Motor and General Motors. Automobile manufacturing was no industry for late bloomers, or so it appeared. Hundreds of competitors had come and gone by then, and those few who still remained in the race were running far behind the two leaders. Had the new company not been headed by Walter Percy Chrysler, few in the business would have given a second thought to the chances for the Chrysler Corporation to succeed.

The auto industry discovered Chrysler in 1911 and he was already 36 years old. Compared to Henry Ford and William Durant, the two men whose respect he would later command, he was a novice in the business. Chrysler already had realized and far surpassed his childhood goal of being "the best doggoned machinist on the railroad." He had risen through the ranks and held a top production job with a locomotive manufacturer. Persuaded that he could make as strong a mark in the automobile business, Chrysler was lured to General Motors. Once on the automotive scene, his genius was quickly recognized, richly rewarded and eventually widely sought.

Born on April 2 of 1875 in the small town of Wamego, Kansas, Walter Chrysler was raised in a family headed by a passenger train engineer and developed an early fascination with machinery. Riding with his father in the cab of the locomotive during runs was a treat to which he always looked forward, but even more exciting was being around the railroad shops and roundhouse in Ellis, Kansas — the railroad town his family moved to while he was still young and where Chrysler spent most of his youth.

By the time Chrysler was 17, his heart was set upon being a machinist. He had finished high school and was already working in the Ellis railroad shops, sweeping floors. He also was an avid reader of Scientific American, the bible for all who took machinery and science seriously. Eager to learn all that he could about machines, Chrysler frequently submitted questions to the magazine and occasionally the published answers would run a column or more. His parents wanted him to go to college and pursue a different career, but young Chrysler insisted he was making the right choice. A machinist apprenticeship soon opened, and he eagerly took it.

Historians disagree over whether Chrysler actually took a five-cent-an-hour pay cut, or received a five-cent pay raise to 10 cents an hour when he became an apprentice. But he would later develop a penchant for accepting less money on a new assignment than he was earning on the preceding job as he was confident that in the long run his performance would enable him to recover any sacrifice made. However, the apprenticeship paid Chrysler considerably less than he needed to purchase the tools of his trade. So, using scrapped metal, he made nearly all of his tools by hand. One exception was a pair of hand-made calipers he accepted with surprise and delight from his father.

From 1892 to 1908, Chrysler roamed the Plains States and the Southwest, carving a niche for himself in his trade. He worked in Willington, Kansas, where he rose to the rank of machinist. Later he did stints in Ogden, Utah, and Cheyenne, Wyoming. In 1901 he took time off to marry Della V. Forker, his boyhood sweetheart from Ellis, and they settled in Salt Lake City, Utah. There he enrolled in a course in mechanical engineering with the International Correspondence School. Soon he moved once again, this time to Trinidad, Colorado, where he became a general foreman. Next he was off to Childress, Texas, where he became a master mechanic earning $160 a month. From there it was on to Oelwein, Iowa, where, in 1908 at age 33, Chrysler became superintendent of motive power at the Chicago Great Western Railway from Minneapolis to Chicago — the youngest man to ever hold the post. This was the same year that Henry Ford introduced the Model-T and William Durant organized the General Motors Company, and Walter Chrysler was bitten by the automobile bug.

Chrysler did not drive automobiles. In fact he did not know how to drive. However, while on one of his frequent visits to Chicago he visited the Chicago Auto Show. There he spotted an ivory-white Locomobile, equipped with red leather upholstery, brass trim and a khaki top. He was completely captivated with the car and had to have it, not for driving but rather to take apart. The Locomobile incorporated many of the mechanical features he had mastered over the years, and he saw in the Locomobile an opportunity to provide the public with locomotives not tied to railroads. Though locomotives would not be his eventual product, vehicles engineered with as much precision would, he believed, be the trademark for his automobiles.

The Locomobile cost $5,000. Although there were no taxes in those days, still the average wage was only about $1 a day for a 10-hour day. Chrysler had long since graduated from the average-pay category. He was earning about $350 a month, owned a home and had $700 in savings. But $5,000 was still a bit rich for his blood. A banker friend of his, Ralph Van Vechten of the Continental National Bank of Chicago, was hounded by Chrysler into giving him a $4,300 loan soon after another of his friends, Bill Causey, was persuaded to co-sign the note. The purchase wiped out Chrysler's savings. Van Vechten, who two years later played an instrumental role in persuading fellow bankers not to scrap ailing General Motors, called the whole deal "madness."

Soon the Locomobile was shipped to Oelwein by railroad and rested in Chrysler's barn. He immediately took it apart, studied it, and then carefully put it back together. He repeated the routine over and over several times until Chrysler was convinced he completely understood how it worked. After devoting hours to studying the Locomobile, Walter Chrysler had convinced himself that he was ready to build similar machines. At this time, he also quit the railroad quite abruptly after being criticized, unnecessarily he felt, by the railroad's new president. His boss was eager to apologize and get him back to work, but instead Chrysler wired an old friend who had become the president of the American Locomotive Company in Pittsburgh. The friend hired Chrysler, and eventually made him the manager of the company's Pittsburgh works. In under 15 years, Chrysler had risen from a broom pusher to a builder of one of the greatest machines of all time, the steam locomotive. With his new job, which eventually paid $12,000 a year, Chrysler paid off the bank loan in Chicago and immediately purchased a second car.

Chrysler's work at American Locomotive was soon

recognized by those in influential positions, one being James Jackson Storrow. A director of American Locomotive, Storrow was also the chairman of the finance committee of General Motors and head of Lee Higginson and Company, a Boston investment banking firm. Storrow had been appointed head of a group charged with reviving General Motors in the aftermath of its 1910 brush with disaster when Durant overextended himself the first time. In establishing a new management team, he asked Chrysler to join General Motors as works manager under Charles Nash at the prestigious Buick factory in Flint. Chrysler was thrilled at the opportunity. The job only paid $6,000, a year, half of what Chrysler was then making, but he accepted it anyway.

General Motors had closed all of its plants except its Buick and Cadillac operations. Both cars had gained reputations for quality and the future of the company seemed to rest on their success. When Chrysler took over Buick manufacturing in 1912, only 45 cars a day were being produced. In contrast, the Ford Motor Company was turning out 1,000 cars a day. Chrysler faced the challenge and took a variety of steps to improve production, which included the discarding of the traditional carriage-making assembly method. He established moving production lines based on techniques developed at Cadillac and Ford Motor and in the process became a stickler for engineering excellence. Soon Buick was humming again. Three years after Chrysler set foot into the Buick works, its sales increased to 140,000 units, and between 1910 and 1915, Buick and Cadillac accounted for virtually all of General Motors' profits. During the next five-year period Buick sales alone supplied half of the auto company's profits.

While Chrysler was upgrading Buick, he was also taking note of his own personal stock. Feeling the oats that many thought were reserved only for such industry czars as Ford and Durant, Chrysler one day in 1914 marched into the offices of Charles Nash and demanded

a salary of $25,000. Nash nearly choked. He had become
the president of General Motors only several months
after Chrysler was hired. Knowing Chrysler's worth he
readily gave into the demand. Then, just as Chrysler
was leaving the office, he added that he would want
$50,000 the following year. This time Nash nearly fainted.
But Chrysler knew that he was worth his weight in gold
to the company.

A year later, in 1915, when Durant regained control
of General Motors, Chrysler was besieged by Storrow to
leave the company and join Nash, who had resigned to
form Nash Motors in Kenosha, Wisconsin. Later Nash
merged into what is today American Motors. Chrysler
declined the offer, explaining that he did not want to
move his family again. Meanwhile, Durant attempted to
assure Chrysler's continued presence at General Motors
by promoting him to the presidency of Buick, and
boosting his salary to $500,000 a year. Chrysler also
demanded full authority over Buick and was made first
vice president of General Motors in charge of manufacturing
operations. The uneasy relationship between Chrysler
and Durant, whose first love at General Motors had
always been Buick, did not last long. Durant resumed
his free-wheeling tycoon business practices which had
brought the company to its knees less than a decade
previous. Chrysler, the head of a company responsible
for earning nearly one half of General Motors' profits,
and fearful that it might all end in ruin, quarreled with
Durant over his loose business dealings. Unable to resolve
their differences, Chrysler retired from General Motors
in 1919 at the age of 45. A millionaire with a reputation
as one of the best manufacturing executives in the
industry, Chrysler's retirement would not last long.

Within the year, Chrysler was approached by a
committee of bankers who had collected some $50 million
in loans that were in jeopardy at the Willys-Overland
Company. The small automaker was experiencing extreme
difficulties during the post-World War I economic slump

and the bankers desired Chrysler to run the company for at least as long as necessary to recover their money. Chrysler was hesitant to stake his reputation on this new rescue. But to Chrysler's surprise Ralph Van Vechten, the Chicago banker who 12 years earlier had loaned Chrysler the $4,300 to buy the Locomobile, was among the bankers soliciting his help. Chrysler agreed to take the job for $1 million, net.

Once the Willys effort was underway, the bankers persuaded Chrysler in 1921 to also sort out the problems of the Maxwell Motor Car Company, another respected name in the business which was also on the brink of collapse. Maxwell owed the bankers between $26 million and $32 million, depending upon the historical source. Hesitant to tackle the much more difficult Maxwell quagmire which also involved the Chalmers Motor Car Company, Chrysler held out until John N. Willys added his voice to the bankers. Chrysler agreed to take the post of chairman of a management committee that would reorganize Maxwell and Chalmers. Ironically, this time he asked for only $100,000, plus options on a big block of stock.

While working out the Willys financial problems, Chrysler met the engineering team of Zeder, Breer and Skelton. Fred M. Zeder was a graduate of the University of Michigan and had worked for Studebaker. Owen R. Skelton was a graduate of Ohio State and had worked for Pope-Toledo and Packard. Carl Breer was a Stanford graduate who had worked for Allis Chalmers. The trio, which came to be known as the "Three Musketeers," eventually became the nucleus of Chrysler engineering. Each was ahead of his time when working individually for several automakers. They had joined forces and formed a consulting firm in Newark, New Jersey whose ideas strongly impressed Chrysler — they were much like his own. He solicited their help in reorganizing Willys, and by 1922 the job was complete. The bankers arranged for a $10 million bond issue to retire the outstanding loans, and the company was put into receivership while its affairs were worked out.

Meanwhile, under a reorganization plan that included the Maxwell and Chalmers interests, a group of lenders subscribed to $15 million of new money to those two companies. The creditors received two-thirds of their claims paid in one, two and three-year notes of a proposed new company, and one-third paid in cash.

With Zeder-Skelton-Breer, Walter Chrysler had found a team that would help him produce a generation of distinctive cars with a new standard of engineering excellence which became his company's trademark for decades. The first test of the combined efforts of Chrysler and his engineers was ready by the end of 1923. It was called "The Chrysler Six." It was the nation's first medium-priced automobile equipped with a high compression engine, resulting in better performance. It also featured hydraulic brakes, providing greater breaking power. It had replaceable oil filters, aluminum pistons, shock absorbers and other unique features. The Chrysler Six launched the Chrysler Corporation, offering consumers features that had previously been available only to luxury-car buyers.

The Chrysler Six made its debut in New York City at the Commodore Hotel in January, 1924, at the New York Automobile Show. It was an instant hit. The Maxwell Motor Company received orders for 32,000 Chrysler Sixes, a record for first-year sales of a new car. On the heels of this success, Maxwell Motor's business and property was transferred to a new company, the Chrysler Corporation, founded on June 6, 1925, and headquartered in Highland Park, Michigan. The Chrysler Six outsold the Maxwell three to one, and the latter was soon discontinued. By 1927, the Chrysler Corporation was the fourth largest automobile manufacturer in America.

While Walter Chrysler sought to build automobiles with excellent engineering that would sustain his reputation in the marketplace, he also was hard at work assembling a management team to help steer his company. A credit to his financial genius was his hiring of Bernice Edwin "B.E. " Hutchinson as treasurer of Maxwell. "B.E.," as most knew him, for once an adult he never used his first name, was recommended to Walter Chrysler by some Wall Street friends who had been watching the Chicago native work a little magic in reorganizing a failing paper company in Massachusetts. His tough hand on the cookie jar lid reigned for years and Hutchinson retained control until his retirement in 1954. Chrysler recruited former General Motors cohort Kaufman Thuma Keller in 1926, who took charge of manufacturing and later emerged as a dominant figure of the Chrysler Corporation. Keller, who preferred being called "K.T." remained with Chrysler until his retirement in 1956. Marshaling the engineering efforts into the 1950's was one or more of the original members of the Zeder-Skelton-Breer team that developed the first Chrysler car.

Around the same time, 1935, a teenager who migrated to Detroit from Scotland with his family amid thousands of others seeking work in the booming new industry was getting his feet wet in the grimy factories at Chrysler. Douglas Fraser, who worked in the DeSoto plant and was the son of a line supervisor at Chrysler, never dreamed then of having the influence over the future of the Chrysler Corporation which Walter Chrysler and his team had had in the company's first decade. But Fraser grew to see the company from another perspective and years later shuddered to think how long things would have continued as they were, and of what actions were required to change them. Likewise, in 1942, Marc Stepp, found his way to Detroit from deep in Indiana and was assigned a lowly task in the factories, not knowing that, along with Fraser, he too would be rewriting automotive history.

The early years of Chrysler Corporation's success were rounded out in 1928 with its acquisition of Dodge Brothers, Inc., for about $100 million in stock, plus the assumption of $59 million of Dodge debt. Almost since Detroiters first became interested in making cars, John and Horace Dodge had been making components for automakers, including Ford Motor, General Motors and others. In 1914, they established Dodge Brothers Inc., and began making automobiles themselves. Both died in 1920, the victims of an influenza epidemic that swept the nation. Their company sustained itelf on its sheer momentum, but when that began to run down, it was offered to Chrysler. The Dodge purchase increased Chrysler's physical size five-fold, and gave the company access to another solid set of new-car dealers. In the same year, Chrysler's Plymouth and DeSoto, two highly successful and comparatively low-priced Chrysler cars, were launched. Chrysler cars were oft-times priced higher than those of General Motors, but the company operated on the premise that one out of four persons would choose superior engineering.

Between its strength as an innovative automaker and the shortcomings of its opponents, Chrysler became one of the Big Three by 1929, and by 1936 it displaced Ford Motor as the second largest auto company in the nation, behind General Motors. Despite a dramatic drop in the industry's sales during the Depression years, Chrysler emerged in 1936 debt-free and in command of 25 percent of the retail passenger car market. The company at this time also developed a new engineering approach called "Airflow." Unfortunately, it was so far ahead of its time that it flopped, but like so many other good ideas it was later adopted by the entire auto industry. With its reputation as an innovator well established, Chrysler did not lose its hard-won second place position until 1950, when the Ford Motor Company staged a dramatic design comeback in the marketplace.

By 1935, Walter Chrysler was literally burned out.

At peace with and proud of his tireless years of work and achievements, Chrysler turned the presidency of the company over to K.T. Keller on July 22, 1935, only 10 years after he had launched the venture. He remained the chairman of Chrysler Corporation until his death, but was not again active in the company's management. He moved, once again, to New York, where he became severely ill in 1938, soon after the death of his wife. Chrysler never recovered from that combination of blows and on August 18, 1940, he died of a cerebral hemorrhage at age 65.

Reprinted from Fortune Magazine, photo by Pictures Inc.

Walter Percy Chrysler, at left, the kid from Kansas who wanted to be the best mechanic on the railroad, turned out to be one of the best executives in the automobile business, a career that climaxed with the founding of the Chrysler Corporation. Kaufman Thuma Keller, at right, succeeded Chrysler, and is said to be the man under whom the fall of the Chrysler Corporation began. Like his predecessor, Keller always wore a hat and vowed that as long as he ran the company it would not make cars with rooflines so low that a man could not sit upright in one with his hat on.

Chapter 4

"*We build cars to sit in, not piss over.*"   K.T. Keller

K.T. Keller's election on July 22, 1935 as president of the Chrysler Corporation ended months of speculation over whom Walter Chrysler would select as his successor. Several top company executives had been considered in the running. Among them was Bernice Hutchinson, the financial wizard of the company, who felt his engineering and production background, his work since 1921 in assembling financial packages to underwrite Chrysler projects and his prudent decisions during the Depression that guarded the company from disastrous financial competitors, were certainly worthy of merit. There was Fred Zeder, who led the engineering team that put Walter Chrysler's ideas on wheels and then kept them fine-tuned. Zeder also savored the thought of a crack at the top spot. Finally, there was Keller, the gutsy factory genius, who banked his chances on his close and long-time relationship with Walter Chrysler, as well as his proven abilities in the factory and front office.

All three contenders were strong-willed men and

had demonstrated exceptional abilities in their respective areas of work. Each had considerable knowledge of the others' fields, and under Walter Chrysler's strong and intense leadership they worked well together to achieve his goals. At times however, they found themselves competing in trying to influence the direction of the company by vying for Chrysler's attention and, later, his chair. Sometimes it appeared to be a draw. They made it a practice, for example, to meet Walter Chrysler jointly at the Detroit train station upon his returns from frequent business trips to New York City on the Detroiter, a luxury train that had won a reputation of being the auto executives' traveling club. As a group, they were eager to hear Chrysler's news.

Perhaps because Keller's experiences were a close reflection of Walter Chrysler's own career, namely an American success story of rising from rags to riches and from factory to the front office, he ultimately chose Keller to be his successor. Time would show that this reflection was, in many respects, merely an illusion.

The reign of K.T. Keller over the Chrysler Corporation management team to which the wary Walter Chrysler entrusted the future of his automobile company would span over some 20 crucial years. Their finest hours, however, would be tied to the Chrysler Corporation's successful involvement in World War II. The praise that was to be bestowed on Keller and his associates for their tireless and profitable efforts overshadowed other developments for some time, beginning the decline of the Chrysler Corporation. From 1935 to the end of his undisputed rule in 1956, Keller presided over the Chrysler Corporation's transition from an aggressive and innovative corporation under Walter Chrysler, to a company fiscally conservative and slow to update its cars. Chrysler followed trends rather than set them.

Keller, who had earned his spurs first in the factories at 20 cents an hour and worked his way to the front offices where his salary grew to six figures, was in many ways like his predecessor, Walter Chrysler. Born November 27, 1885, in Mount Joy, Pennsylvania, Keller, like Chrysler, was fascinated with machinery from an early age. In his efforts to be a machinist, Keller moved to Pittsburgh to enroll in a two-year apprentice program run by the Westinghouse Machine Company of Pittsburgh, the forerunner of the Westinghouse Electric Company. It was a good move. Soon after his graduation from the program, he found work as the superintendent of the automobile engine department at Westinghouse.

At the age of 24, Keller moved to Detroit to seek his fortune in the city that by then had become the hub of the American automobile industry. He made the rounds, working at Metzger Motor Car, Hudson Motor Car, Maxwell, General Motors, and the Cole Company. Keller returned to General Motors where he became master mechanic at Buick. It was there he met Walter Chrysler who later claimed to be instantly impressed with Keller's grasp of his work.

Just as Chrysler had, Keller climbed the corporate ladder at the big automaker, becoming the vice president in charge of manufacturing at Chevrolet and then the general manager of General Motors' Canadian operations. But in 1926, Keller turned in his keys to the management washroom at General Motors, and, at the request of his old friend, Walter Chrysler, joined the small but ambitious Chrysler Corporation.

Keller was an excellent technician in the image of Walter Chrysler. His first assignment was as the vice president of manufacturing at a time when the company was bubbling with new cars and engineering innovations at a pace oft times ahead of consumer demands. Tackling the hard jobs would become Keller's forte. As a testament to his efficiency, Chrysler historians emphasized his work in consolidating the Chrysler and Dodge manufacturing operations after the Dodge division was purchased by the Chrysler Corporation in 1928. Less than 90 days after the establishment of a team to improve the Dodge operations, the factory space required for manufacturing at Dodge was reduced by one half and the surplus space was used to make the new DeSoto car.

Keller's tenure, first as president and then as chairman of Chrysler, immersed him in nearly every facet of the company's affairs, welcome or not. At the headquarters he consumed himself with such trivia as making certain that only initials were used in the company directory and on office doors, thus the source of "K.T." Keller, "B.E." Hutchinson, and "F.M." Zeder and so on. It was not until after Keller died that most of those who worked under him for years learned his full name, Kaufman Thuma Keller, and by then few cared. The idea of using initials suited Hutchinson even more. From the day he began work at Chrysler, he never used his first name, Bernice, and long after his death one of the trivia questions at Chrysler was, "What was B.E.'s name?" In the factories Keller occasionally insisted on personally supervising the arrangement of new equipment, often delaying the completion of an installation for months.

On the executive level, Keller wrestled with Hutchinson over the financial chief's philosophy about spending money. It was wise, Hutchinson insisted, to take advantage of profitable years to fatten investor dividends and executive salaries, and then spend only what was necessary to maintain and upgrade production facilities. Keller eventually subscribed to that philosophy.

Dabbling in the styling and engineering departments was also a Keller practice, despite the authority held over these departments by Zeder and his associates. A noticeable by-product of their relationship was that after the war Chrysler emerged with a philosophy that cars could look as stodgy as they had before the war, so long as they were well engineered. There was never any certainty of just who the Chrysler customer really was, only the faith that consumers desired a well-engineered automobile. More often than not, most of Chrysler's customers came from the nation's blue collar masses who wanted dependable transportation that would last for years. That trait was associated with Chrysler more than with its major competitors.

Refusing to follow the styling trends of the industry after the war may have been a personal decision as well as a business one for Keller. A robust, barrel-shaped man who always wore his hat in the plants and at his desk, Keller insisted that Chrysler should not build cars with rooflines so low that a man wearing a hat could not sit upright in one. During a new car preview in the early 1950's, Keller was asked why Chrysler did not follow its competitors and lower the rooflines: "We build cars to sit in, not 'piss over," Keller is said to have answered.

The impact of Keller's policies on Chrysler began during the war effort when in June, 1940, he received a phone call from Lieutenant General William S. Knudsen, director of the Government's Office of Production Management. Knudsen had resigned as president of General Motors in order to take the government post. Why he chose to call Keller is unknown. But Knudsen wanted to know whether Chrysler could produce a new tank in quick order. A meeting between Keller and Knudsen resulted in an affirmative answer after just five minutes of discussion.

Within eight months, Chrysler had built a huge military tank production plant in Warren, Michigan, a small town just north of Detroit, and was producing test models of the new M-3 tank. As the war effort shifted into high gear, Chrysler along with its competitors landed dozens of war production contracts and mothballed their automobile production for the civilian market until the war tapered off in late 1945 and early 1946. The list of Chrysler's war sales was the envy of any manufacturer: 25,000 tanks, 438,000 army trucks, 18,000 B-29 superfortress engines, 60,000 Bofors anti-aircraft guns, 7,888 "Sea-Mule" marine tractors and tugs, 29,000 marine engines, 101,000 incendiary bombs, 20,000 land mine detectors and 1,000 train car loads of atomic bomb manufacturing equipment.

Between the tanks and materials for assembling the atomic bomb, Chrysler won a permanent place in the American military production establishment. In the process, K.T. Keller emerged from the war as decorated as anyone who had risked a life on the battlefields.

President Harry F. Truman, who had become a close friend of Keller's during the war when Truman was a Senator heading a panel investigating waste and inefficiency, saw to it that Keller received the Medal of Merit for his distinguished service during the war. Keller, a 32nd degree Mason, also became the first industrialist to receive the Gourgas medal, the highest decoration of the Scottish Rite Order of Masons. The most impressive of all honors came to Keller in October, 1950, just a month before his election as chairman of Chrysler Corporation. He was appointed the director of the Government's guided missile program, a position he held until late 1953.

The end of the war triggered the beginning of a new golden era for the American automobile industry. After 1946, public demand for cars outstripped supply, and for a time most automakers simply dusted off their mothballed production equipment and churned out pre-war model cars. Chrysler was no exception; only it practiced the billing of old models as new ones longer than its major competitor, Ford Motor.

The Ford Motor Company was still a privately owned family business, but it had undergone sweeping changes at the top in 1945 when young Henry Ford II emerged as its head after the bitter family struggle caused by the rapid deterioration of the company's founder and the rapid fiscal decline that accompanied it. Ford Motor was losing millions of dollars daily and many feared that it would sink into bankruptcy unless a new management designed a quick turn-around plan. As the war came to an end, a group of Air Force officers at the Pentagon, who had become familiar with Ford Motor through their dealings with the company during the war, privately voiced their great concern to Henry Ford II. They offered to help overhaul the company.

Once in control of the company, Henry Ford II hired the team which wanted to help out. Among the group, initially referred to as the "quiz kids" and later known as the "whiz kids," was Charles B. Thornton, who later left Ford Motor to work for the Howard Hughes organization and then founded his own company, Litton Industries; J. Edward Lundy, who rose to be an executive vice president; Arjay Miller, who eventually served as president of Ford Motor, and Robert S. McNamara, who was also president of Ford Motor for a stint. Later, McNamara served as America's Secretary of Defense in the Kennedy and Johnson administrations and then became president of the World Bank. While the group was being groomed, Ford II recruited Ernest Breech, a General Motors executive, to help map out an immediate reorganization plan to restore Ford Motor's financial health and to produce new products to unseat rival Chrysler. Between 1946 and 1950, Ford Motor spent $2 billion on plant modernization and capacity expansions. The new cars were unveiled in 1949 and became an instant success.

At Chrysler, meanwhile, the company's top management decided to ride the post war boom for as long as it lasted without spending heavily on plant improvements or making dramatic changes in its products. This tactic seemed well founded, particularly since Chrysler was selling cars as fast as it could make them. The post-war sales boom produced some of the highest profits in Chrysler's history — $62.7 million in 1947, $89.2 million in 1948 and $132.2 million in 1949, all records. The spiraling profits kept the dividends flowing, but masked real problems in the making.

In each of those impressive years, Chrysler's share of the industry sales had diminished. Something had gone wrong and little, if anything, was done about it. From a 25.7 percent share of market sales in 1946 — the first full year of civilian passenger car production after the war — Chrysler's share of sales slipped to 21.8 percent in 1947; 21.5 percent in 1948; 21.4 percent in 1949, and 17.6 percent in 1950.

Ford Motor during this time, charged with new zeal and punch, registered an 18 percent share of the market in 1946; 21.1 percent in 1947; 18.8 percent in 1948, 21.3 percent in 1949, and 24 percent in 1950. That year Ford Motor toppled Chrysler from its position as the nation's second largest automobile manufacturer, a blow from which Chrysler would never recover.

The Ford Motor victory over Chrysler was helped by yet another Keller move that most, in retrospect, view as a serious mistake. Keller decided to take on the United Automobile Workers. By then, the industry had been negotiating with the U.A.W. as the collective bargaining agent for its factory workers for over a decade. A negotiating pattern had been established as far as the Big Three manufacturers were concerned; what the union won from one company, it got from all three. It was absurd to think otherwise, particularly during a boom period such as that the industry experienced in 1949 and 1950. But Keller refused a union proposal for funding pensions, a plan already accepted by Ford Motor and General Motors. The union struck Chrysler on a cold day in January, 1950, and the strike lasted 100 days. When it was over, Chrysler had lost over $1 billion of production and had accepted essentially the same pension plan that it had rejected earlier. Keller received no honors or decorations at the end of 1950. Though the company earned an impressive $127.9 million that year, Chrysler had not only given up its competitive edge to

Ford Motor in the marketplace, but also lost its respect at the bargaining table. Aside from turning a profit in spite of itself, the only other good thing Chrysler did that year was to elect Lester Lum Colbert as its president. Keller became chairman, a position through which he retained a firm hold over the company until his retirement in 1956. But the change at the top signaled an opportunity to plow new ground before the company's position eroded further.

Colbert (pronounced call-bert) was called "Tex" in honor of the small Texas town of Oakwood where he was born on July 13, 1905. People there remembered him as the youngster who, while still in elementary school, worked at the soda fountain of the local drug store and organized his classmates to help him run a laundry route. Years later, he was admired by the nation's business and financial power brokers as the architect of the modern Chrysler Corporation. Colbert, who was discovered and hired by Walter Chrysler himself, would indeed set the stage for a Chrysler Corporation comeback.

Colbert's early aptitude for business was nurtured by his mother, a school teacher; as well as his father, a small-time cotton planter and buyer who operated a general store in Oakwood. By the time Colbert was 13 years old, he had begun to master the art of cotton buying and dreamed of the day when he could sink his teeth deeper into the business. By the age of 16, he had earned enough money during summer breaks to pay his way through college. He attended the University of Texas, graduated at 19, and was accepted at Harvard Law School. He later admitted that he did not spend enough time on his law school studies, and after he graduated the law school dean was unwilling to find him work in New York City as was the tradition for all students with "good grades." Colbert argued with the dean that despite his grades he knew his law and would be a good worker. It did no good. So Colbert asked a classmate to write down the names of the top five law firms in New York and then paid them visits alone. Of the five firms, all filled with Harvard graduates, one threw him out and two said they might hire him. The one that finally did was the law firm which did the legal work for Walter Chrysler's family and the company.

Colbert's first assignment was to handle some odd work for Walter Chrysler's son-in-law, who had a small business in Pennsylvania. His performance was impressive, and soon he was assigned to handle various lawsuits in which the company was involved. During that time, Nicholas Kelley, a partner in the firm and the person who had helped Walter Chrysler organize the company in 1924, surprised Colbert with a message that Walter Chrysler himself wanted to meet him in his New York office at the Chrysler Building. Colbert found the walls of Chrysler's cluttered office lined with penny clocks; Chrylser was fond of collecting them. The conversation was brief, but to the point. Between draws on his cigarette and pleasant bursts of profanity, Chrysler explained that he wanted Colbert to come to Detroit and set up a legal department within the company. Colbert asked for five days to think it over — not because of fear of reprisal from Kelley or any doubts that he could handle the task. He had planned to go back to Texas and work in his family's business after a few years in New York. Going to Detroit was not in the cards, so he thought. However, with the blessings of his childhood sweetheart and wife, Daisy, Colbert agreed and became the first in-house attorney for the Chrysler Corporation.

Within a few days, Colbert was aboard The Detroiter along with Chrysler, who treated the young attorney to his first train ride via the sleeper car. The journey was highlighted by sips of contraband whiskey that Chrysler had stored in his plush train suite and rounds of chatter lasting until the early morning hours with several General Motors executives also on board. When Chrysler and

Colbert arrived at the station in Detroit, they were met, as usual, by Keller, Hutchinson and Zeder.

Colbert focused first on labor relations and the manufacturing operations. To sharpen his understanding of various jobs, he learned to operate several tools in the factories and later, at Keller's encouragement, attended night school to study blueprint reading. He soon became a vice president and a member of the board of directors of the Dodge Division. World War II found Colbert in charge of building and operating the huge Dodge war plant in Chicago where the Wright 18-cylinder airplane engines were built. Working against near impossible deadlines, Colbert ran the construction of the plant on a 24-hour basis like a field marshal in combat. During the winter, when the weather was so bad that one could barely get about at the construction site, he hired 25 horses from an area riding academy so supervisors could span the 500-acre site on horseback. Colbert's relentless effort to complete the building and turn out the aircraft on schedule reminded fellow workers at times of a scene of the Roman Emperor driving his slaves.

In 1945, at the end of the war, "Tex" was rewarded with the presidency of the Dodge Division. There, at the age of 40, he supervised one out of every three Chrysler Corporation employees and witnessed first-hand the execution of policies that would lead to a quick Chrysler slide. Keller and Zeder were slow on style changes for the cars, and "Hutch", as the stuffy financier liked to be called, was just as slow in loosening the purse strings. New models were not exactly new; they always had basically the same flair from 1946 to 1953, despite a limited overhaul in the late 1940's. These models sold on the sheer strength of the booming market. But it was all a dream world, and Colbert knew it.

Colbert had a chance to leave Chrysler with an offer from Henry Ford II in 1948 to join the ambitious effort to turn Ford Motor around. But at the suggestion of Keller, for whom Colbert had considerable respect,

File Photo from the Chrysler Corporation

Lester "Tex" Colbert was the architect of the 'modern' Chrysler Corporation, presiding over the company's transition to an ambitious style and marketing organization with a more modern plant.

the offer was politely declined. The next year, Colbert was elected a vice president and director of Chrysler. Then, in the fall of 1950, Colbert received a surprise phone call from Keller advising him that he would be named president of the company. His official duties started November 3, 1950.

The new president of Chrysler quickly learned that as long as Keller remained on the scene there were some things that he, Colbert, would not be allowed to change. The same stagnancy held true in financial matters with Hutchinson at the controls. But when Colbert sternly argued that profitability was never to be gained as long as the company continued to use outdated production methods and equipment, he was able to wrestle nearly $1 billion out of Hutchinson for plant modernization. Then in 1954, Colbert won a $250 million 100-year loan at 3.75 percent interest from the Prudential Insurance Company of America.

Colbert also persuaded a reluctant Keller to allow a confidential management study to be done by McKinsey & Company, a prestigious consulting firm. Years later, in the late 1970's, the same firm would also be used by Henry Ford II, to help determine the future course of the Ford Motor Company and who should lead it after his retirement.

Colbert was warned that McKinsey would take a year or two to write a six-foot-tall report, that it would cost a bundle of money, and that probably no one would ever read it. McKinsey employees spent hours looking over shoulders at Chrysler, interrogating workers and challenging their ideas about the company. When they had finished their sweep through the company, McKinsey dropped the bomb.

The report, as thick, detailed and costly as Colbert had been warned, delivered a scathing attack on the Zeder-controlled, Keller-dominated schools of engineering and design. If the company was to regain its competitive spirit in the marketplace, the report concluded, the stodgy, boxy cars designed by Fred Zeder and later by his younger brother James, would have to be scrapped. The report further advised that Chrysler would have to assume an international dimension if it was to regain its prestige. Ford Motor had been plowing ground abroad almost since the day that Henry Ford began making the Model-T. General Motors, while moving more slowly, also had interests abroad. The report also suggested ways to improve the company's financial management procedures. In all, there were literally hundreds of recommendations covering the entire organization and despite the predictions, it was read.

Long before the McKinsey documents were delivered, Colbert suspected what might be suggested. Some events to help speed their implementation had been started. For one, Hutchinson retired in 1953. The authority of James C. Zeder, who succeeded his older brother at his retirement as the czar of engineerng and styling, was whittled away by Colbert as Virgil Exner, a stylist hired from Studebaker in 1949, was given increasing responsiblity for styling plus an express pass to the offices of the president and chairman. Exner, who began moving Chrysler out of the boxy-car era with the 1955 "New Look" cars, was the first stylist at Chrysler who was able to tell Keller to scrap an idea and actually get away with it. Some Chrysler veterans, Colbert included, later would say that the impact of the McKinsey report caused James Zeder to have a stroke in 1956, the year he died. Keller also retired in 1956, and Colbert assumed the chairmanship of the company in addition to the presidency.

Exner, by 1956, was hard at work on a line of cars that would symbolize Chrysler's last substantive bid to challenge Ford Motor for second place. The cars, introduced in the 1957 model year, would spark an industry trend toward rear-end fins and breathe new life into Chrysler sales.

Tragedy struck Chrysler in 1956 with the untimely

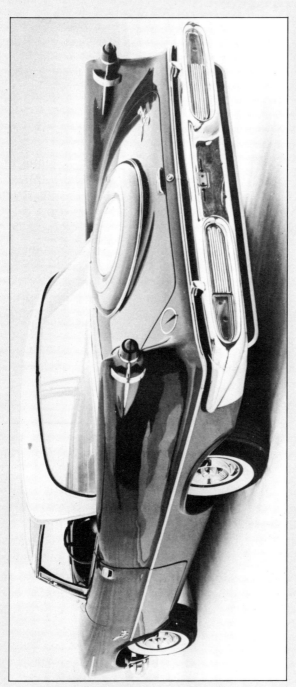

File Photo from the Chrysler Corporation

The 1957 Imperial included sweeping tail fins, integrated gunsight tail lights, massive wraparound rear bumper and enlarged glass areas.

deaths of three of the company's key operating officials
— all within six months. Carl J. Snyder, vice president
for manufacturing, went down in a plane crash; Cecil
B. Thomas, vice president for international activities,
died of a leg injury, and George W. Troost, vice president
for finance, never recovered from brain surgery. Colbert
had his hands full in trying to fill the newly opened
positions and at the same time provide the staffs to
back them up. One person recruited was Lynn A.
Townsend, a cocky young accountant described by his
boss as the best man in the Detroit office of Touche,
Ross & Company, the accounting firm that did Chrysler's
outside accounting. Townsend, who had worked on the
Chrysler account at Touche, Ross for 10 years, was
appointed controller at Chrysler in 1957. In searching
for other replacements, Colbert came to fully realize
another Chrysler weakness: there were a few good people
at the top, and few below were ever groomed to succeed
them.

Colbert took the McKinsey recommendations quite
seriously, especially the suggestion that Chrysler expand
its horizons worldwide. He began by making the prestigious
Rolls Royce an offer. It was promptly rejected because
Rolls Royce was, and always would be, British, he was
told. He tried to buy Volkswagen, then a small German
automaker. But Heinz Nordhoff, the head of Volkswagen
from 1948 until his death in 1966, discouraged Colbert
from pursuing the purchase. He explained that it would
be almost impossible to identify the shareholders of the
operation since the government, once the primary owner
of VW, had distributed the shares to the people. Lawsuits
by unknown shareholders would cramp such an acquisition
effort for years, Nordhoff advised Colbert. He also made
a dollars-and-cents argument. Volkswagen held less than
five percent of the world market at that time, Nordhoff
added, and he did not see Volkswagen ever growing to
the point where it would be as economical to build and
sell cars in the United States — then a key growth

market — as it was to build them in Germany and then sell them. Undaunted, Colbert kept overseas expansion high on his list of priorities for rebuilding Chrysler and before his departure the objective began to bear fruit with the purchase in 1958 of an interest in Simca.

Asked once after his retirement to describe Walter Chrysler, Colbert characterized him as "an eternal optimist. He would never accept defeat." It was in that spirit that Colbert found himself struggling during the 1950's to restore the Chrysler Corporation's prestige and financial strength. As the decade ended however, he would ponder a puzzling trail of events that successfully led the company out of the dark ages but failed to restore it as a growing company with a flair for competition.

The updated manufacturing operations helped improve the company's profit per vehicle, although it was still far behind that of General Motors and Ford Motor. Colbert took the labor bull by the horns as well, and cut 30,000 factory workers from Chrysler's bloated heydays payroll. In the marketplace the popular fin cars of the 1957 model year worked like a spring tonic and brought praise to Colbert for his efforts. Sales soared in 1957, giving Chrysler an 18.3 percent market share and a profit of $125.1 million.

Things soured for the company just about as fast. Rushed into production a year ahead of time in order to cash in on the still booming market and bring to the fore a distinctively new Chrysler style, the new models turned out to have numerous structural flaws and rampant rust problems. In the next year, 1958, Chrysler's sales slumped 50 percent. Its reputation for engineering quality flew out the window and it lost $29.6 million. In 1959, Chrysler was caught in the recession that swept the country and, despite trying to make amends for its poor fins, it had a loss of $2 million.

More disheartening was the fact that despite the biggest boom decade the industry had ever experienced, Chrysler's market share continued to erode. When Colbert assumed the presidency, the company had a disappointing 17.6 percent of the market. Ten year later, in 1960, when he relinquished the presidency, Chrysler's market share had fallen to 14 percent, making it a distant third. Ford Motor's share had risen to 26.6 percent. Foreign cars, non-existent before 1950, commanded 7.6 percent of the market.

In yet another recovery effort, Colbert appointed William C. Newberg, his protege, president on April 28, 1960. But a stock holder's allegations of a conflict of interest on Newberg's part due to his involvement with other businesses, led to his abrupt dismissal two months later.

Newberg had substantial interests in two small companies that did business with Chrysler, and a Detroit attorney, Sol A. Dann, owner of a substantial number of Chrysler shares, dominated stockholder meetings and jammed Detroit court dockets with lawsuits charging Newberg and others with conflicts of interest. Colbert was never linked to any of the activities, but with some encouragement he recognized the need to clear the air and try once again to bring in fresh blood. He relinquished the chairmanship and presidency of the company on July 27, 1961. Colbert was too young to qualify for the company's pension program. So in traditional corporate style, he received another assignment — chairman of Chrysler of Canada — for a year until he reached retirement age.

Newberg, whose holdings in the outside suppliers had always been somewhat a matter of public knowledge, did not take lightly the loss of his chance to head Chrysler. He had worked for the company for 20 years. As a farewell, he surprised Colbert, his mentor, with an appearance at the exclusive Bloomfield Hills Country Club. The meeting resulted in a scuffle that was the talk of the town for some time, but never saw the light of day in Detroit's major newspapers. The Newberg dismissal and Colbert's decision to leave touched off a scramble to find new leaders for the company. The search would be led by George H. Love, a Pittsburgh coal executive whom Colbert had met on a trip to Florida and in 1958 invited to serve on Chrysler's board of directors. While the search for a new president went on, Lynn Alfred Townsend, the bean counter who had been shaking things up at Chrysler, became administrative vice president of the company in December of 1960.

Townsend was an often arrogant, sharp-tongued man who had developed a reputation at the company as a cost-cutter. That was not all that Colbert and Love were searching for in a chief executive but their efforts to recruit a top man of their own choosing did not yield positive results. Edward M. Cole, the General Motors engineer who was general manager of the Chevrolet Division, and Semon E. Knudsen, general manager of the Pontiac Division of General Motors, were on their list. Knudsen was a son of the late Lieutenant General Knudsen, who presided over General Motors just before the start of World War II. Between January and July of 1961, Cole, Knudsen, and several others were queried. All turned down the top spot. As a last resort, Townsend was selected and appointed president on July 21, 1961.

An ambitious man, Townsend was "the best man around who would accept the job," as a former Chrysler executive familiar with the selecton put it later. The Flint, Michigan native, born May 12, 1919, would cause people to shudder before he was to leave 15 years later, and the reaction started as soon as "L.A. Townsend" could be inscribed on the door of his new office. As administrative vice president, he faced a fact Colbert had refused to deal with, that the company was far too fat personnel-wise on the management side. To cure that financially draining situation, Townsend ordered the immediate dismissal of 7,000 white collar workers, about 15 percent of the total salaried work force. The move, which saved the company $50 million annually, was brutal. In contrast to the treatment given ousted senior executives, no consideration was given to the few weeks or months which employees had to go before pension time after dedicating the best of their years to the company. Engineers and research workers were swept out along with secretaries and obscure sales representatives. Lynn Townsend shrunk the "big family" as Chrysler had come to be known. But his methods were detested.

Soon after Townsend became president, Love was elected chairman of the board. His elevation, in September, 1961, was extremely significant. For one thing, as chairman of the Cleveland-based M.A. Hanna Company, at the time the nation's largest closed-end investment trust, and as chairman of the Consolidation Coal Company, the nation's largest coal producer, Love had impeccable credentials in the business community and a reputation for a no-nonsense approach to business ventures. Also, Hanna, built by Love's predecessor, George Humphrey, who had served as Secretary of the Treasury in the Eisenhower Administration, operated on the principle of not taking lead roles in companies without having some financial interest in them. As a result, Consolidation Coal, in which Hanna owned a substantial interest, purchased a block of Chrysler stock. That move was soon followed by the purchase of a small block by interests representing the Rockefeller family. Much of the success of General Motors and Ford Motor had been attributed to the fact that there was some party involved in those companies holding a large enough block of stock to whip management into line whenever it seemed to be without direction. Many hoped the same thing would now happen at Chrysler.

During this transition period, a confidential study of Chrysler was done for the Consolidation Coal directors in late 1961 by outside consultants, this time Loomis, Sayles & Company. It served as the white paper used to pursuade Consolidation Coal to acquire an interest in Chrysler. However, the Loomis findings were, in effect, a New Testament reaffirming the tales of the old.

"In recent years, inept management has hurt the company's competitive position and adversely affected earnings," said the report. To support that observation, it reviewed Chrysler in the post-war years.

Chrysler's competitive position and volume had shrunk from over 20 percent of industry sales in 1946 through 1953 (except for in 1950) to an average of 14 to 15 percent in the years 1954 through 1960, Loomis said. In conjunction with that, the number of Chrysler dealers had dropped to about 5,500 in 1961 from about 10,000 in 1954. The shrinkage was, in part, the result of a deliberate effort by the company to eliminate many dealerships in cities where there were too many in business for any to make reasonable profits. But as part of the whole dealer problem, the decline of the ranks of dealers went too far. Another problem documented was the "trend toward radically styled or ostentatious models" that had received good consumer acceptance in only one of the past six years. Finally, it said, the company had suffered from "sharply reduced" earnings in a majority of the years after 1953 — with only two good earnings years out of eight.

Despite the discouraging past, Loomis beamed, "There is a real place in the industry for a strong 'number three' company." It concluded that with the right action from the front office, Chrysler had impressive long-term growth potential, and that on the basis of prevailing cost-price relationships, Chrysler could earn from $13.00 to $23.00 a share, assuming an 8 million unit passenger car sales year for the industry and command of a market share of between 13 and 17 percent. (Some 5.5 million units were sold in 1961 and by 1965, sales totalled 9.3 million units.)

Townsend was taking all of the right steps, the Loomis report said, noting that in several conversations with him since 1957 "he has always impressed us favorably as knowing the problems of Chrysler, (and) as being realistic and determined to solve them."

Townsend's background may have been strictly numbers, but his broad sweep would be felt all through the company in many different ways. He had adopted a "new policy" of adjusting the company's production costs and the size of its organization to the realities of its share of industry sales, then 12 percent. The Loomis study noted this policy was aimed at putting a $2.5 billion business on a profitable basis at the earliest possible date. Chrysler's revenues rose a bit in 1968 to $2.6 billion, with earnings equal to more than $28 a share based on the 9 million shares outstanding when the Loomis report was made. But by 1968 there were 46.9 million shares of Chrysler stock outstanding and per-share earnings that year were $6.48. In addition, a new chief designer, Elwood P. Engel had been hired from Ford Motor. In contrast to his strong-armed predecessors, Engle would develop new products through a group effort with emphasis on establishing at Chrysler "a consistent style that is evolutionary rather than revolutionary," as the Loomis report put it. To build a stronger dealer sales body the Chrysler board authorized an investment of up to $300 million in loans for the following 10 years. Virgil Boyd, a top salesman at American Motors, joined Chrysler and successfully managed the Chrysler dealer body.

To shore up the company's tarnished reputation for quality, Townsend backed up Boyd and the now-growing number of Chrysler dealers with a new five-year, 50,000-mile warranty. And to present a new image of Chrysler, Townsend hired a company to develop a new corporate trademark.

In executing the many plans, Townsend gained a reputation for secrecy and having an over-active ego. For example, the new corporate trademark, the penta star, was a total surprise to company officials. Developed by Lippincott & Marguilies, a prestigious New York consulting firm, the penta star was the cornerstone of an entirely new corporate identity program launched by

Townsend and cost Chrysler in excess of $50 million. Similar secrecy prevailed around a corporate organization plan that he sprang on his associates one day, having quietly declined to use the corporate planning group charged with that task. Despite Chrysler's size, when Townsend joined the company, it did not have an organization chart. Townsend also kept three sets of sales projections: low ball, high ball and middle set. The low ball would go to investors, the high ball to sales executives and the press. But the middle set stayed in his vest pocket. Those were the real numbers.

No dust was gathering under the shoes of Chrysler in other areas. It maintained its Government ties as the nation's only developer and producer of combat tanks. The tank business was a small one compared to others in which Chrysler was active, but it was always profitable and a vital link to Washington. Chrysler likewise made a big splash in the space program during the 1960's, as it had in the war effort of the 1940's. It landed Government contracts early in the space programs and was instrumental in the production of the Redstone missile. Between 1961 and 1975, Chrysler built 31 launch vehicles that were used for various space programs. Chrysler achieved a 100 percent success record with its launch vehicles.

Under Townsend, Chrysler also established numerous other profitable subsidiaries, such as Chrysler Financial Corporation, Chrysler Realty and Chrysler Insurance. These all proved to be winning ventures and, with the McKinsey study in mind, Townsend forged ahead with an expansion of the company's international business. By the end of the 1960's, Chrysler had established itself as a multi-national company. It was building automobiles through wholly owned or majority-owned auto companies in 11 countries and selling them in over 100. The investment required to attain such an enviable position in the industry was $500 million.

With the 1958 acquisition of 25 percent interest in Simca, from Ford Motor and Italy's Fiat, Simca became

Chrysler's foundation in the international marketplace. It spread its wings wherever it could find the room, including Spain, England, Australia, South Africa, Turkey, Argentina, Brazil, Columbia, Peru and Venezuela. The success of the Simca deal is a wonder, considering how it began. Negotiations for part of the Simca stock were conducted in French and Italian. The only member of the Chrysler entourage who fully comprehended all that was being said, it was learned later, was a Chrysler public relations official. "If Townsend knew what was being said, he would never have bought Simca," the aide commented later. But, as is the case with powerful executives, once Townsend had made up his mind to do something, no one dared disagree. Meanwhile, the company's operations in Canada, where Chrysler had been doing business since its founding, were beefed up. By the mid-1960's, Chrysler reported that over 20 percent of all its vehicles were manufactured outside the United States, with more than 30 percent of its vehicle sales the result of transactions outside the United States. Townsend had become an internationalist much as the Ford family had been for decades, particularly under Henry Ford II. At Chrysler, Townsend equated circling the globe with manifest destiny, even if it required using funds that might better have been spent to improve the product at home.

President Townsend's magic, backed by George Love's work on Wall Street and Virgil Boyd's work in strengthening the dealer body, seemed to have worked.

Between the cost-cutting moves and growth in new business programs and products aimed at restoring Chrysler's respect, the company was placed in step with the rest of the industry. Spreading Chrysler cars around the globe made its financial reports pretty reading. Profits soared to $65.8 million in 1962, from $9 million in 1961. In 1963 they hit $163.4 million and in 1964, $215.4 million. In 1965, the year the nation's news media staged its own publicity blitz hailing the return of

Lynn Townsend marshalled a revival of the Chrysler Corporation in the 1960's that prompted many in the automotive community to declare the company back in the running as a viable automaker. But the empire he built collapsed and Townsend was forced to retire in 1975.

Chrysler to prosperity, the company reported a $239.5 million profit. Its market share rose to 15 percent, the highest since 1957. In 1966, the final year of Love's service as chairman of Chrysler, profits dipped to $194 million, but they rebounded in 1967 to $203 million. In July, 1967, Townsend was rewarded with the chairmanship of Chrysler and Boyd with the presidency. Love, having achieved his mission, returned full time to his other interests.

In 1968 profits rose to $302.9 million — a record. Chrysler's employment in the United States rose to 140,204 people in 1968 from its decade low of 74,000 in 1961, the year of the payroll massacre. The company's market share reached 16.3 percent.

In the late 1950's, Forbes Magazine had labeled the American automobile industry "the Big Two and a Half," the latter being Chrysler. But as the company rebounded, Townsend basked in his success by boasting of the new Big Three — "G.M., Ford, and Me."

The Chrysler rebound had another side for those who viewed Chrysler from a global perspective, assessing its leaders, operations, products and competitors. A nagging question remained: How deep did Chrysler's recovery really run? The reasons for their concern were numerous.

At home, many of the right things had been done but the only real difference about the "number three" automaker was the great distance between it and its competitors. Its products were more in tune with the times but still depended upon the success of sales tides rather than carrying their own weight. Management responsibilities were spread among more people, but the company still remained basically a one-man operation under Townsend, and little grooming was taking place to compensate for any abrupt changes in leadership.

In addition, Big Brother, in the form of General Motors, kept reminding Chrysler who was the boss in the automobile business. In 1965, 1966 and then again in 1967, Chrysler raised its prices on new cars only to have General Motors refuse to follow suit, thus forcing an embarrassing Chrysler rollback. Chrysler was still farming out more of its work and making fewer cars than both General Motors and Ford Motor, meaning its per-car costs were higher than those of its competitors. Artificial price ceilings, such as those dictated by General Motors, only frustrated Chrysler's profit plans via higher vehicle prices.

Abroad, the heralded overseas expansion was characterized by many as being about 30 years too late in blossoming, forcing Chrysler to pick from among the leftovers in many instances. "Simca was a wise move," observed Harvey E. Heinbach of Merrill Lynch Pierce Fenner and Smith, the nation's largest brokerage house. "But Rootes cost them a bundle." When Townsend broached the idea of purchasing Rootes Motors Limited in England back in the mid-1960's, even "Tex" Colbert, who had wooed Rolls Royce, communicated his skepticism over the wisdom of such a move saying he did not see great potential in Rootes. But he had long since become a part of Chrysler history and simply another of its shareholders.

The big problem in being stuck with one or two good foreign operations and a multitude of leftovers was that Chrysler could not smooth out the bugs in its overseas network. Revenues increased yearly during the 1960's, but profits went up and down like a yo-yo. If Rootes of England required little attention, then Brazil did. If not Brazil, Australia. If not Australia, Venezuela. Sometimes problems emerged at all four operations. Before Rootes was sold by Chrysler in 1978, Chrysler had lost over $200 million in its attempts to keep it afloat. The money spent by Chrysler was in addition to some $330 million the British Government pumped in during the mid-1970's through its subsidies after Chrysler threatened to withdraw and let the company collapse.

Chrysler was also hurt by the rising sales of imports

during the 1960's. General Motors and Ford Motor felt much less of this sting. Although Chrysler was a worldwide company, it was a weak one at best.

Another major concern to many, both inside and outside Chrysler, was Lynn Townsend himself. Sometime during 1965, middle management began to feel he was becoming bored. As the 1960's drew to a close, Townsend spent more and more time in activities outside the company. He became a fund raiser for the Republican party in the Middle West and in 1970, as a highlight of his civic involvement, he became the chairman of the National Alliance of Businessmen. The "evolutionary" styling that was a hallmark of Townsend's management began to slip, and Chrysler cars seemed to return to the stodgy, boxy look of the early 1950's while those of General Motors and Ford Motor became sportier. Fear of dropping back in the race began to permeate the company again.

It was the fall of 1968 when the worst fears about the weakness of Chrysler began to crystallize. From the moment that the new 1969 model-year cars rolled into the showrooms, Chrysler's headquarters complex in Highland Park was abuzz with worry that the roof was about to cave in. They did not know then how right they were.

In 1968, Chrysler introduced a whole new line of its full size cars which included the Imperial, Chrysler, Plymouth Fury, and the Dodge Polara. These sharp cars, some of the largest automobiles introduced for the 1969 model year, were greeted with distinct disinterest by a car-buying public which suddenly preferred a smaller car or nothing at all. To make things worse, 1968 marked the beginning of a recession, a development whose impact first hit the bulk of Chrysler's patrons — blue collar Americans. Chrysler was in a near panic.

Resorting to tried and true methods, Townsend immediately laid off 11,300 of Chrysler's 140,000 workers. Among the victims were several hundred people trained in production work under the government's JOBS program, an employment training project actively supported by the National Alliance of Businessmen. Townsend slashed Chrysler's operating budgets three times during that year and halted construction work on a new assembly plant as business became progressively worse. (That facility was later bought by Volkswagen as its first American assembly plant.)

Townsend also ordered Chrysler's 1969 models immediately overhauled for the coming model year, something that normally would not have been done until the 1972 model year. To demonstrate that management was also prepared to be disciplined for the traumatic experiences of 1969 and 1970, Virgil Boyd was removed from his post as president. Company profits tumbled to $99 million in 1969 from the $302.9 million made in 1968, but the dividend remained untouched at $2.00 per share, the same amount that Chrysler had paid during its considerably more profitable three previous years.

Chrysler emerged from 1969 traumatized. That it was so badly shaken from a single year slip-up in the marketplace while the nation's economy was in a brief slump demonstrated its vulnerability and confirmed quiet speculation that the empire which Townsend had built rested on a fragile foundation. Suddenly Townsend was scrambling to protect his reputation as a financial wizard in the face of challenges from within the company — from his traditional domestic competitors, plus foreign competitors, lenders, shareholders and the growing crop of Government regulators who all began to surface during the 1960's.

Townsend's partner in battle was John J. Riccardo, a 45-year-old accountant and alumnus of Touche, Ross. Ricccardo had joined Chrysler in 1959 and, under Townsend's wings, he had been catapulted through a series of key sales positions in preparation for a time when he might lead the company. Smaller in stature than Townsend, Riccardo built a reputation within the

Photo by Tony Spina, chief photographer, "The Detroit Free Press."

In the early 1970's, John J. Riccardo, (pictured above) then president of Chrysler, had some of his best years in the automobile business ahead of him, or so he thought. By the middle of the decade, Lynn Townsend, his mentor at Chrysler, would heed the suggestions of Riccardo and others, to retire and after a mild scramble in the board room, Riccardo would emerge as the new chairman of the company. By 1979, he would follow in the footsteps of his predecessors, leaving the company at a low point that would overshadow whatever positive contributions he might have made.

company as being one who knocked on heads instead of desks when trouble arose. What distinguished Ricccardo from Townsend, in the minds of many subordinates, however, was his willingness to put more time into solving problems after identifying them. On January 8, 1970, Riccardo was elected the president of Chrysler, and Boyd was elected vice chairman. Boyd's election was largely ceremonial, and preceeded his retirement from Chrysler on September 30, 1972.

Townsend had calculated that between himself and Riccardo, the two bean counters would turn Chrysler around once again. However, as the 1970's progressed, it became evident inside the executive suites at Highland Park that nothing short of a bailout could save the Chrysler Corporation.

On the heels of the profits slump of 1969, Chrysler lost $7.6 million in 1970, its first yearly loss since 1959. Townsend and company finally bit the bullet and reduced the shareholders dividend to 60 cents for the year, from the $2.00 proudly paid out in each year since 1966. In that same year, American manufacturers launched a half-hearted show of strength against the increasing sales of small, low-priced foreign cars. General Motors began marketing the Vega while Ford Motor introduced the Pinto. Chrysler, unable to finance a small car of its own, began distributing a line of small, low-priced imports in 1971. The cars, made by Mitsubishi of Japan, would compete more profitably with the General Motors and Ford models. General Motors is said to have never made a sustained profit on the Vega and Ford Motor's Pinto was always a financial loser. Chrysler, in third place in the industry, would have fared worse had it tried building its own car then.

Lenders also put the squeeze on Chrysler in 1970, after being thrust into a near panic over the bankruptcy of the Penn Central Transportation Company. In June, when the giant Eastern railroad company filed for bankruptcy with debts running into the hundreds of millions, lenders who dealt in so-called "commercial paper" began plowing through their portfolios looking for other American businesses that could be next in the bankruptcy line behind the Penn Central. Chrysler surfaced as the No. 1 candidate. (Commerical paper is a promisory note a borrower gives the lender for a short-term loan, which can run from one day to 270 days. Funds raised this way are often used to pay off another loan due.)

The Chrysler Financial Corporation, the dealer financing arm of Chrysler, was a heavy user of commercial paper. In fact at that time it was trying to sell over $1 billion in such notes. Lenders retreated fast. It took the personal involvement of John McGillicuddy of Chrysler's lead banker, the Manufacturers Hanover Bank in New York, plus behind-the-scenes arm twisting by the Federal Reserve Bank to avert a total run on Chrysler financially, one that bankers later said could have been fatal to the parent company. It was months later, though, before Chrysler Financial recovered from the events precipitated by the collapse of the Penn Central.

By the 1971 model year, Chrysler had a newly designed line of intermediates ready. The market had shifted again, this time back to full-sized cars, but Chrysler's size and product lines had been adjusted and now however briefly there was the feeling that Chrysler had to ride it out.

However, less than two years later, by the fall of 1973, it had capsized again. Just as Chrysler was introducing a whole new line of full-size passenger cars for the 1974 model year, war broke out in the Middle East. The Organization of Arab Petroleum Exporting Countries (OAPEC), a group possessing and exporting a goodly portion of the oil commanded by the larger Organization of Petroleum Exporting Countries, imposed an embargo on oil shipments to the United States. By then America was importing some 40 percent of its petroleum needs, compared to zero at the start of World

War II. The embargo, which lasted four months, triggered a stampede for smaller, fuel efficient cars in the United States. All the American manufacturers could offer was a handful of small, relatively fuel-efficient cars; overall, sales nose-dived. As fuel supplies tightened up, gasoline sales techniques which had not been used since World War II began to emerge. Stations sold gas only during the day and then only on weekdays. They limited the amount which could be purchased at any one time. In addition, some states restricted gasoline purchases by requiring drivers to match their odd or even license plates to odd or even days for fuel purchases. And finally, the speed limit was eventually reduced nationally from 75 to 55 miles per hour on interstate highways.

These events happened just as Chrysler launched its new line of full-size cars. Disaster had struck again. Chrysler's losses in 1974 amounted to $52 million. Townsend's final act before leaving Chrysler was to swing the ax again. Between 1974 and 1975, he removed 30 percent of the company's workforce, including 80 percent of its engineering department, from the company payroll. Ford Motor also had a house-cleaning but to a lesser extent, as did General Motors. Like Chrysler, Ford Motor canceled or postponed some domestic car projects. But General Motors, in a rare move, opted to borrow $600 million and thus kept some of its new car product programs alive.

Townsend spent most of 1975 struggling to hold up his head as he told everyone who asked that he would stay on until the bitter end. In the opinion of many onlookers, the end was at hand. Sure enough, Chrysler's profits continued to nosedive through 1975, its market share shrank to under 12 percent, and Townsend abruptly retired in October, 1975, leaving Riccardo with a sinking ship. Chrysler's business at home and abroad was on the skids. The year ended with Chrysler reporting a 1975 record loss of $259.5 million. Just as chilling was the suspension of all stockholder dividends for all of

1975. It was the first suspension since 1933, which had affected only two three-month pay periods.

Washington, meanwhile, had become obsessed with the desire to take more decisive actions on the energy front beyond a reduction of the speed limit in retaliation against those who dared threaten the nation's mobility. Among the maze of energy conservation laws cranked out was a get-tough approach for reducing the consumption of gasoline by automobiles, which at the time represented 40 percent of the nation's gasoline consumption. Legislation was passed ordering American automakers to reduce the gasoline consumption of their passenger cars. The Congressional conference committee that resolved differences in the versions of the new energy legislation, ordered a 100 percent improvement in the average fuel economy of American-made passenger cars to 27.5 miles per gallon by 1985 from just under 14 miles per gallon in 1974.

It was the most monumental task assigned the industry since World War II, and required the complete retooling of the nation's automobile business — in short, rebuilding American-made passenger cars from scratch. They would have to be smaller in size, weigh thousands of pounds less in some cases, and operate on about half the power in 1985 than they did in 1975. Despite the immensity of the task, Washington felt confident that Detroit could handle the job. In its decades of growth, the industry had built its reputation along the theme of "we can do it."

In reality, to comply with the fuel economy mandate from Washington required enormous resources and few had looked recently at the balance sheets of such companies as Chrysler and American Motors. Chrysler had been in the forefront of other battles with the Government, particularly over an emerging trend toward the regulation of the automobile industry. It argued vigorously against a law mandating mileage standards and campaigned instead for voluntary programs sanctioned by then-President Ford. Fear prevailed at Highland Park that should Chrysler's fortunes not change in the near term, the weight of the revolutionary changes being mandated from Washington could bankrupt the company.

Unfortunately for Chrysler, its arguments had become far too familiar in Washington and overall the industry was still alive and well. The Chrysler appeal fell upon deaf ears as Washington decided that firm action was needed fast, and knew of Detroit's track record for delivery of the impossible.

"Taking over the chairmanship at that time, we knew that down the road we were going to have some very serious problems." Riccardo recalled later in an interview. "So our whole approach was to see what we could do as quick as we could and that meant to get as liquid as we possibly could."

Riccardo knew that Chrysler would be begging for trouble if it sought help from the outside before it did all that it could internally to raise funds. The master plan was to tighten up and dispose of everything possible in order to salvage its business in North America.

"Anything that doesn't pertain to our defense business or North American automotive operations has to go," Riccardo told his executive corps. Within hours a dramatic dismantling of Chrysler had begun.

Abroad, Riccardo began by immediately dismantling Chrysler's international operations, getting whatever funds possible and pouring them into North American retooling. By early 1979, Chrysler owned interests in only two foreign companies outside North America, specifically, 15 percent of PSA Peugeot-Citroen, the largest automobile manufacturer in Europe, and 15 percent of Mitsubishi Motors Corporation, the Japanese automaker whose subcompact cars Chrysler had been selling since 1970.

At home, Chrysler divested itself of its Airtemp air conditioning operations, a substantial portion of its real estate holdings and other miscellaneous operations deemed non-essential to becoming a strong North American automobile company. For model year 1976, it rolled out its first post-embargo cars, the Aspen/Volare compact series. The cars helped sales rebound, but like the fin cars of the 1950's they turned out to be trouble-prone; the result of being hurried into production. The two cars became the most recalled models in Chrysler's history. The engineering reputation of Chrysler was again damaged and many customers vowed never to buy another Chrysler product.

During the same time that Riccardo was divesting the Chrysler Corporation of nearly everything but its plumbing, he also called upon the company's lenders. It started, in fact, before Townsend's departure with Riccardo's visits to 40 American lenders considered essential to the company's fiscal well-being, plus a handful of Canadian bankers.

"It was particularly important," Riccardo recalled later, "in light of the Penn Central railroad bankruptcy in 1970. The banks bailed Chrysler out then." Between 1976 and the summer of 1979, Riccardo visited the 40 American banks on three different occasions, trying to keep them attuned to Chrysler's increasing needs.

Chrysler surfaced above water in 1976 and 1977, riding the tide of a post-embargo sales boom. It posted a $422.6 million profit in 1976, a $163.2 million profit in 1977. But the company began going under again in 1978 when heavy expenditures for new tooling wiped out the gains in sales of some products, particularly trucks, which netted the company a good profit and sold well. That year, Chrysler lost $204.6 million, and began sending smoke signals to Washington about its looming ills.

Totally unsuspected, however, was the fall of the Shah of Iran in the spring of 1979. The new Iranian Government imposed an embargo on oil shipments to the United States, and although it was only a small share of all imports, it triggered a replay of the 1973-74 stampede for the most fuel-efficient cars available, and the rationing of gasoline sales throuugh alternate-day sales of fuel in some parts of the nation. Aside from its Mitsubishi cars and one new subcompact line of its own, Chrysler again had a wide array of products its customers did not want, including vans, trucks, and big down-sized cars. Chrysler reported a first quarter 1979 loss of $53 million, and a second quarter loss of $207.1 million. With the prospect of the year's losses totalling $1 billion and no new sources of revenue in sight, Riccardo yelled bailout.

Chapter 5

"Voluntarism? Ha, Ha...."
                    Senator Maurine Neuberger, Oregon:

It came as a shock to most who heard it for the first time. Riccardo, one of the nation's leading industrialists and free enterprisers, wanted the government of the United States to salvage failing Chrysler. There were two reasons for this decision, although only the latter commanded considerable public debate.

First, every major source of private money in America as well as several abroad, most notably Volkswagen of West Germany, had refused to lend a hand to the drowning company. American lenders claimed they had extended enough to Chrysler — more than $4 billion — and were at their prudent, if not legal, lending limits. Volkswagen, while in search of additional capacity to meet the swelling demand for its new line of vehicles in the United States, saw little merit in establishing a major working relationship with Chrysler despite their long-standing business ties. (In addition to purchasing Chrysler's New Stanton, Pennsylvania, assembly plant, the German automaker had supplied the engines for

Chrysler's first small-car era automobiles, the Omni and Horizon). At home and abroad, those possessing the private resources to give Chrysler a needed shot in the arm, stood back, looked at the world automobile industry as they saw it evolving in the 1980's, assessed Chrysler's potential, and then hung their heads.

Second, Riccardo firmly believed that the government had a hand in charting the demise of Chrysler, despite the dozens of mistakes by the company over the years that resulted in its shrinking percentage of sales. There was no conspiracy, he would hasten to add. But, by mandating that all automakers, regardless of strength, tote the same load of government regulations at the same pace, a scenario was developing in which the weak one's were being crippled.

It was a Catch-22, Riccardo argued. The cost of complying with the maze of government regulations, especially those covering fuel economy was about the same for everyone. Recovering those costs was a different story. General Motors made more cars than all of its American competitors combined and thus was able to spread its costs over more vehicles, he pointed out. General Motors, in effect, dictated pricing policy in the marketplace; its smaller competitors were forced to absorb more of the government-mandated costs internally in order to maintain consumer price appeal. The result was that Chrysler realized much less of a profit from each car sold than did General Motors and Ford Motor.

Chrysler's rising costs and its shrinking position in the marketplace were forcing both ends against the middle, Riccardo found. With his private sources shunning the idea of backing Chrysler any further, he had no alternative but to look toward Washington or to bankruptcy court. Pursuing Federal help, he argued, made sense because it was the government that had raised the stakes of the game with its multitude of regulations; safety, clean air, minimum crash damage, noise and fuel economy, and thus the government should share the costs.

By the late 1970's, government regulation was considered the American automobile industry's number one enemy. It was not always this way.

Prior to the 1960's, the automobile industry enjoyed the luxury of being the only major transportation industry in America that was not woven into the web of government regulations. Railroads, air lines, inner city and interstate bus lines and trucking companies all grew with government regulations. What apparently distinguished the automobile industry from the crowd for so long was the fact that the automobile was considered personal property, on the level of a home. As such, few dared to violate the personal freedoms accorded to those who purchased an automobile for their own use. Probably just as important, Detroit and Washington considered themselves partners in progress, a relationship reinforced during times of international conflict. As a team, Detroit and Washington defended the nation during times of war and helped Americans enjoy it during times of peace. Each appeared to respect the other's power and strength, with Detroit possessing as much influence at times over public policy in America as Washington. At least many industry power brokers such as Charles Wilson, president of General Motors from 1941 until 1952, felt that way. Wilson, who left Detroit to become Secretary of Defense in the Eisenhower Administration, told a Senate committee in 1953: "What's good for the country is good for General Motors, and what's good for General Motors is good for the country."

As the nation sought to digest Wilson's cocky declarations, the stage was being set to challenge them. The 1950's took the auto industry to new horizons in its sales of vehicles and saw its political muscle flex as never before with adoption by Congress in 1956 of the Federal Highway Act. This act resulted in the construction of 42,500 miles of Federal interstate highway by the end of the 1970's at a cost to taxpayers of $60 billion in addition to the destruction of thousands of neighborhoods.

But the 1950's was also a decade in which Detroit's role in public health and safety was questioned. Two developments sparked the fire.

In 1953 Arlie Haagen-Smit, a scientist at the California Institute of Technology, confronted auto industry executives with findings that automobile emissions were a major element in the form of air pollution peculiar to the Los Angeles area. He called it "smog." When hydrocarbons (HC) and nitrogen oxides are emitted from automobile engines among other sources as unburned fuel and are mixed with air and sunlight, the result is a photochemical oxident, he found, or smog. It irritates and causes a burning sensation in people's eyes, causes respiratory problems, and looks ominous in the sky. Thus the movement to impose some sort of regulations on automobiles to protect public health got underway.

Three years later, in 1956, Kenneth Roberts, a U.S. Representative from Alabama, planted the seeds of a movement to regulate automobiles to enhance public safety. Roberts, although a true believer in state's rights and minimum government intervention, began focusing on automobile safety as chairman of the new House subcommittee on traffic safety.

Although Haagen-Smit's discovery touched off a multitude of subsequent studies, including one launched in 1954 by a team of industry scientists, and the Roberts Congressional hearings stimulated increased sensitivity to the subject of automotive safety, support for their efforts was slow in coming. Public apathy and low-keyed, but persistent efforts by the industry to persuade government to allow the manufacturers to adopt voluntary standards to address health and safety concerns worked against the would-be reformers. It was not until 1964 that the two men saw light at the end of the tunnel. That year, the California Air Resources Board imposed the nation's first mandatory standards governing allowable exhaust emissions from automobile engines, and Congress adopted a bill directing the General Services Administration to establish minimum safety standards for the automobiles purchased for use by government employees.

By the mid-1960's, the nation was engulfed in a mushrooming consumer rebellion that rivaled the civil rights movement in momentum. As the civil rights movement had spread, the consumer movement also quickly moved into the spotlight with the automobile industry at the core of its concerns. The movement grew in part because of the boom in car sales of the 1950's, with over 75 percent of the nation's households becoming automobile owners. And, as prices increased, the automobile emerged as the second largest single purchase an individual would make in a lifetime, after a house. Apart from those factors, concern was mounting over the national highway death toll — running close to 50,000 fatalities a year — a number which appeared to rise as the use of the vehicles spread.

Detroit had survived numerous challenges to its "voluntary standards" stance. But in Washington, the automobile safety advocates were amassing their forces for a showdown with the industry, one that would stir a hornet's nest before it ended.

At issue was whether the American automobile industry could or should continue to wield enormous power over American transportation policy, public health and safety without some sort of government regulation on behalf of the people. The industry resented the entire idea of regulation, recalled Rodney W. Markeley, Jr., a retired Ford Motor Company vice president who became the first auto industry representative to register as an auto lobbyist in Washington.

"The basic idea of this being a large inbred industry, and the concept of the sun rising on the East side of Detroit and setting on the West side of Detroit, groomed a great reticence against being roused," Markley would recall.

After the Roberts hearing, a second era of debates over Federal regulation of the automobile industry began in March, 1965, with hearings by the Senate Subcommittee on Executive Reorganization. Senator Abraham Ribicoff of Connecticut, the committee chairman, was a real traffic safety buff. As the Governor of Connecticut, he ordered the licenses of drivers ticketed for speeding to be suspended in an effort to reduce highway fatalities. Through his hearings, which ran for a total of only 10 days and were spread out over an extended period of time, Ribicoff sought to sort out what the Federal Government was doing in the area of traffic safety.

Senator Ribicoff was assisted in his committee hearings and investigations by a young Connecticut lawyer, Ralph Nader. An auto safety advocate himself, Nader was then writing a book on the Chevrolet Corvair, a small car introduced in 1960 that incorporated several innovations, including an air-cooled engine positioned in the rear of the car.

At Nader's urging, the Ribicoff hearings not only probed the Federal Government's role in traffic safety, but also put the auto companies on the spot by examining what they were doing to improve the safety of their vehicles and exploring such sacred turf as how much money was spent in the effort. Nader became so inspired during the Ribicofff hearings about the need to publicize the industry's indifference to auto safety that he sped the completion of his book.

Released late in fall of 1965, *Unsafe at Any Speed* finally roused the public and put the issue of automobile safety in the limelight. By Christmas it had sparked numerous forums in Washington addressing the auto safety regulation issue, and only few were pro-industry forums. In addition to Ribicoff's subcommittee, a group of freshman representatives on the House Commerce Committee, led by James Mackay of Georgia, began drawing up a bill to regulate the industry. A chief aide to Mackay was Joan Claybrook who emerged in the late 1970's as the chief Federal Automobile safety enforcement official as administrator of the National Highway

Safety Administration. Meanwhile, the Lyndon Johnson Administration, recognizing the inevitable, prepared a proposed legislative package over the Christmas holidays to send to Congress after the New Year, forwarding it in late February to the Senate Commerce Committee.

Throughout the give and take, the industry maintained that voluntary standards were best. What those standards might have been, no one will ever know. The automakers had political minds as diverse as their individual views on sales strategy, and despite repeated warnings from friends in Washington to adopt a different posture the industry was unable to reach more of a consensus than that it was unitedly opposed to mandatory regulations.

If the industry's ignorance of the way legislation was forged and its inability to compromise on a more realistic position were not enough to seal its casket in the halls of Congress, certainly another shocking development did that job. In secret, the legal department of General Motors hired a private investigating agency to probe Nader. The investigation turned into an embarrassing fishing expedition that intimidated Nader's friends and questioned his personal beliefs on many subjects. As rumors of the startling probe began to be published in the press, Ribicoff was persuaded to hold a final day of hearings, on March 22, 1966, to specifically confront General Motors over whether it had indeed tried to tamper with Nader, who by then had been a committee witness. It is a Federal offense to tamper with Congressional witnesses. That day a bomb was dropped.

Basically that day's hearing was to be limited to testimony by Nader and a representative of General Motors. But Nader arrived late (he said he had missed a cab, but friends commented that he had overslept). As a result, the General Motors witness was called first.

Appearing for General Motors at the hearings, attended by an unusually large crowd of more than 500 people, was James M. Roche, president of the company. He admitted that an investigation had been made of Nader without his knowledge, but said it had started in November, before it was known that Nader would become a witness for the Ribicoff committee. The fact was overshadowed however, by the magnitude of the admission:

> *"While there can be no disagreement over General Motors' legal right to ascertain necessary facts preparatory to litigation, as I shall discuss in a moment, I am not here to excuse, condone, or justify in any way our investigating Mr. Nader. To the extent that General Motors bears responsibility, I want to apologize here and now to the members of this subcommittee and Mr. Nader. I sincerely hope that these apologies will be accepted. Certainly I bear Mr. Nader no ill will.*

> *"When I first read in the press on March 6 that Mr. Nader was apparently being shadowed and investigated, and his friends questioned about his beliefs, I was just as surprised and disturbed as all of you must have been. Two days later, in the process of ordering a formal statement denying our involvement, I discovered to my dismay that we were indeed involved. I immediately ordered an investigation and release of the facts as we then knew them.*

> *"We earnestly hope, Mr. Chairman, that you will not interpret this episode as reflecting GM's response to the issues raised by your subcommittee and by others concerned with traffic safety. We deeply share that concern. We want to consider all complaints and suggestions on their merits, not on the basis of personalities. We know that any automobile is subject to accident and that we must be constantly devising and improving ways to protect the occupants and others. If our concern for safety has not always come through with sufficient clarity and vigor in previous statements, including our statement before this subcommittee last summer, than I can assure you that we regret that failure."*

The Roche admission catapulted Nader, a virtual unknown, into national prominence as a leading automotive safety consumer advocate and doomed the industry to regulation forever. Soon after the Ribicoff hearings, the industry made a final bid before the Senate Commerce Committee for mercy and a chance to implement voluntary standards. The appeal was opposed by Henry Ford II, though he allowed one of his officials, John S. Bugas, Ford vice president and chairman of the Automobile Manufacturers Association, the industry trade group, to testify on the industry's behalf. In part, Bugas appealed to the lawmakers to accept an industry alternative to mandatory safety standards (referred to in his testimony as Title I):

"1 A commitment by the four automobile manufacturers to a voluntary action program to improve the safety design of vehicles as rapidly as is feasible, to cooperate fully to this end, to assume responsibility for establishment and adoption within the industry of voluntary industry-wide performance standards for vehicle safety, and to work in other ways for faster progress toward safer highway travel.

"2 Strengthening of the governmental role in protecting the public interest in sound and adequate vehicle safety standards. We propose that the governmental role in vehicle safety standards be strengthened by appropriate legislation to provide a joint Federal-State program — one with Federal participation in and support for a much more effective Vehicle Equipment Safety Commission.

"3 A commitment by the automobile manufacturers to report frequently to the Congress, the Secretary, the Vehicle Equipment Safety Commission, other appropriate governmental agencies and the public on the progress of their voluntary action program.

> "This three-point program will achieve the improvement
> in performance standards for vehicle safety intended
> by Title I, will do so more effectively than Title I,
> and will do so without the very real and serious risks
> that, as we have pointed out, would follow from
> enactment of Title I."

Mr. Bugas' appeal to the committee drew the sharp ire
of many members, including Senator Maurine B. Neuberger
of Oregon who rebuffed the industry by saying "ha, ha"
to voluntary safety standards for the automobile industry
or any industry for that matter:

> "....The automobile industry has been able to have a
> voluntary plan since 1900. Only when pressure comes
> from Congress and we think, from the public through
> us, about any of these problems affecting the general
> welfare, only then we get the sudden desire to "let
> us do it...."

> "...so I say 'ha-ha' for any industry that comes along
> and wants to 'let us do it...' The very fact that the
> automobile industry had not done this since the first
> car rolled off the assembly line, and the fact that
> until the air pollution problem got bad and people
> in various parts of the country got concerned, was
> there any attempt to put bypass devices on the cars.
> So it is lovely to have you volunteer a lot of these
> things, but some of us are skeptical...."

At the conclusion of the day's hearings, it had
become apparent that the industry would get nowhere
with its voluntarism strategy. A meeting that evening
at the home of Senator Philip Hart, a member of the
Senate Commerce Committee, confirmed their worst
fears. A participant in the meeting recalled Hart's firm

position on the industry's efforts. "If you persist with voluntarism I'll fight you. But if you move toward a constructive program as to what you can live with, I'll join you," Hart told the small group. It was a tough position for Hart to take; he was a senator from Michigan. But the industry representatives were smart enough to realize that without the support of legislators from their own state, they would certainly be at the mercy of their adversaries.

By summer's end, the House and Senate voted overwhelmingly to adopt the National Traffic and Motor Vehicle Safety bill (a combination of the Administration bill, Mackay bill, and host of amendments) and a companion bill, the National Highway Safety Act. Together, they established the controversial National Highway Traffic Safety Administration which provided for uniform and mandatory automobile safety standards and Federal enforcement of highway safety programs. Among a host of powers the agency would be noted for was the authority to order auto makers to recall and repair any equipment found defective by government tests. Later their actions resulted in the massive General Motors recall of cars for engine block cracking, the Ford Pinto recall and the Chrysler recall for engine stalling in its Aspen/Volare cars.

The bills were not as tough as safety advocates had sought, but auto executives admit they could have been much weaker if the industry had not lobbied so doggedly for only voluntary standards, and if the General Motors investigation of Nader had not been initiated.

Despite the decisive setback it had been dealt, the divided auto industry retreated to its old philosophy of voluntarism, the crux of every battle plan. It went down in defeat in every major confrontation with Washington until Chrysler was on its knees.

After the skirmish over auto safety, Congress turned its attention next to the clean air and auto emissions dilemma. Throughout the debate on clean air standards,

General Motors led the pack and declared that voluntary compliance with clean air goals was the best avenue. As the debate wound through Congress, General Motors president Edward Cole warned that imposition of stiff standards could bankrupt the industry because of the massive costs involved in changing engine designs to meet the proposed clean air goals. Even with the use of the catalytic coverter, a pollution control device that treated the emissions after they left the engine but before they passed out of the tail pipe, General Motors predicted dire financial consequences to the industy. The Chrysler Corporation was in the forefront of the clean air debate for years and advocated making engine improvements rather than resorting to devices such as catalytic converters.

"My whole point was that whatever clean-up should be done should be through the engine itself," said Charles Heinen, a Chrysler Corporation chemical engineer who spent most of his professional career working on the air pollution issue. Heinen, a student of the Zeder-Skelton-Breer school, maintained that achieving reduced emissions through re-designed engines would take longer than use of such devices as the catalytic converter, but would, in the long run save "the public" considerable money and waste. Platinum, one of the required natural resources of converters, Heinen noted, would have to be imported from a handful of cartel nations, including South Africa. Furthermore, once the cars were junked, so would their converters be, he added.

On a spring day in March, 1970, at a hearing in Sacramento, California, held by the California Air Resources Board with Haagen-Smit presiding, General Motors surprised its competitors again. Cole arose and announced he was tired of the industry being made the whipping boy of the pollution problem. While declaring his determination to remove automobiles from the limelight, the General Motors president made a dramatic reversal in his position of several weeks earlier and said it was feasible to use catalytic converters to reduce emissions to satisfactry levels. Cole, in his one-man campaign to vindicate the industry from the pollution controversy, said that if California would force refiners to make gasoline without lead, his company would meet the state's air pollution standards through the use of converters. " I have no fear of our technological competence to meet the standards for 1980 if the proper fuel is available," he said.

Ford Motor and Chrysler were shocked at his costly offer. But by year's end, Congress adopted the 1970 Clean Air Act, which imposed tough standards on the industry that could be met in the time-frame set forth in the Federal law only through the use of the catalytic converter, a device which General Motors had coincidentally focused its research efforts on.

The final and most expensive of all automobile laws came in 1975 as a result of the 1973 Arab oil embargo. Like a skipping record, the auto companies again cried for voluntary compliance with goals to be set by the government and industry. Compared to what it would cost the industry to retool every plant and car line to improve the fuel efficiency of its cars, the expense to comply with the auto safety and clean air regulations seemed like pocket change. The idea of voluntary goals was warmly received by President Gerald Ford, who had previously served for many years as U.S. Representative from Michigan. But Congress was tired of hearing the industry cry wolf, and passed the Energy Policy and Cost Savings Act by the end of 1975.

The fuel economy laws required a mandatory compliance program aimed at rapidly reducing the consumption of gasoline in America and ordered the auto industry to increase fuel efficiency by 50 percent in its 1980 models, and by 100 percent in its 1985 models.

The program provided for a two-phase compliance schedule. Phase one would be achieved relatively easily by automakers in building their vehicles lighter. It required annual increments of a mile per gallon improvement beginning with the 1978 model year, continuing through the 1980 model year. Phase two required the total redesign of automobiles and the retooling of plants, with an annual improvement of two miles per gallon starting with the 1981 model year and continuing through the 1983 model year, followed by a one mile per gallon increase in the 1984 model year and a half-mile per gallon increase in the 1985 model year.

By most estimates, the fuel economy program would add some $50 billion or more between 1979 and 1984 to the industry's costs of complying with Federal regulations.

With adoption of the fuel economy law, Washington recaptured control of American transportation policy. For the first time in history, Detroit's engineering and product agenda would be defined as much by bureaucrats and lawmakers in Washington by their setting of automobile fuel economy, emission, safety and damage standards, all to be met in the face of legal penalties for failure to do so, as by executives and engineers in Detroit.

As government regulations proliferated, the industry began cranking out as much literature informing the government on its compliance with or complaints about regulations as it did for its customers about its cars. General Motors, for instance, estimated late in the 1970's that between 1974 to 1976, it had spent over $3.5 billion in "complying, and preparing to comply, with regulations imposed by all levels of Government" during that period.

In the course of protesting at every opportunity to "government intervention" into areas that could, in the industry's view " best be handled in the free marketplace," Riccardo's reputation became well established in Washington. His style of talking rather than listening prompted many to characterize him as the auto industry executive in Washington with the political finesse of a bull in a china closet. Riccardo magnified Chrysler's philosophy of doggedly resisting whatever government challenges might be thrown in its path if those challenges were not on the industry's terms of voluntary compliance and threatened to further drain the company's resources. That he sought refuge in the bosom of his adversary during the company's darkest hour would add even more irony to his call for a bailout.

Chapter 6

"Some people throw firecrackers. Others drop atomic bombs."
William O. Bourke

Just as stunning as the stampede for small, fuel-efficient automobiles in the months immediately following the 1973 oil embargo was the near reversal of buying trends once gasoline supplies had stabilized at considerably higher prices. In the busy new-car and truck showrooms across the nation, it was as if the fuel crisis that had traumatized the nation only several months earlier was merely a bad dream that could never again occur. For Detroit, it was a mixed blessing.

With the embargo ended and stabilization of retail fuel supplies, an industry sales rebound began in the spring of 1975. Along with it came a sustained demand for the least fuel-efficient automobiles available, particularly, intermediate and full-size passenger cars, light-duty trucks, vans (Tennessee Cadillacs), and Jeeps. Intermediate and full-size car sales rose to 60 percent of all passenger car sales in 1977, from less than 50 percent during the depths of the embargo months. By 1978, light-duty trucks were outselling passenger cars in many regions of the nation where passenger cars had ruled the marketplace for decades. Curiously, early in the rush toward trucks and vans, the fastest selling vehicle was Chrysler's Dodge van, which was equipped with a 360-cubic-inch V-8 engine.

American automobiles, rejected during the "energy crisis" as "gas guzzlers," had recaptured their place in the hearts of American consumers. The sales of foreign imports, mostly Japanese models that led the fuel-efficiency pack, staggered after reaching new heights during the embargo-sparked stampede, and import dealers found themselves scrambling to unload their excess inventory. So brisk was showroom activity that between 1975 and 1978 passenger car sales rose 31 percent to 11.3 million units, and light-duty truck sales (including vans and four-wheel-drive vehicles such as the Jeep) rose 66 percent to 4.1 million units. During the three model years 1977-1978-1979, the industry, domestic and foreign combined, sold a record 32.7 million passenger cars and 11.8 million light duty trucks to Americans.

Detroit was not exactly sure how to interpret the long-range implications of this flip-flop in buying activity. But it was certainly welcomed. The vehicles in greatest demand during the post-embargo boom just happened to be those that returned the highest profit to their manufacturers, this in comparison with lower-priced compact and subcompact model cars. And the industry was in dire need of billions of dollars to finance the redesigning and retooling of its products and manufacturing plants to build cars and trucks that would meet the tough government-mandated fuel economy standards that would begin with the 1979 model year.

The problem, put simply, was that the boom further dampened what little desire automakers had to build smaller, more fuel-efficient, but less profitable models. In fact, if anything, the post-embargo sales slowed the transition to smaller cars with smaller engines, and hastened Detroit's efforts to weaken the fuel economy standards. There was a genuine fear that short of some dramatic change in the gasoline supply and price situation, the industry would be cranking out 10 million cars the size of match boxes by 1983 to only have them rejected en masse by consumers. That would thrust the entire industry into financial chaos.

The industry's impressive 1978 passenger car sales of 11.1 million units camouflaged the fact that the boom was over and a weakness was beginning to permeate the market place. As it turned out, the strong sales were due almost entirely to the strength of General Motors, which had taken the lead in the downsizing campaign, and to the curious behavior of American consumers, who were defying the traditional laws of economics.

General Motors alone sold 5,385,282 new American-made passenger cars during 1978 in the United States, a record for the company. Its 1978 figures also represented a 5 percent gain over its 1977 passenger car sales and accounted for 58 percent of all American-made passenger car sales in the nation. Meanwhile, sales for Ford Motor rose only 1.5 percent and accounted for 2,582,702 new cars in 1978, while Chrysler sales slumped 5.7 percent below its 1977 figures to 1,146,258 passenger cars.

The consumer role in sustaining 1978 sales was worrisome. Inflation had gradually increased since 1967 and began to skyrocket following the 1973 embargo, fueled in part by a four-fold price increase after OPEC deliveries to the United States resumed prices of imported oil, which were $2.35 to $3.78 per barrel in January of 1973, rose to $11.44, and as high as $15.77 by January 1, 1974. By the late 1970's, inflation was out of control and the government was refusing to impose wage and price restrictions as a tool for cooling it off. Despite the fact that inflaton continued to erode the buying power of the dollar, consumers did not curb their spending as in the past, but rather plunged deeper into debt. The personal savings rate, which began to slow in the mid-1970's, took a nosedive. Savings that had been put away were being tapped as consumers extended themselves further into the credit market hoping to make purchases of automobiles and homes in time to beat the next round of price increases. In addition, Detroit automakers adjusted their pricing strategy by making quarterly adjustments instead of the traditional front-loaded increase at the start of the model years. "Hedge buying" became chic in America.

When another round of oil price rises and the Iranian revolution crushed the big-vehicle sales boom, each auto maker's potential ability to meet capital demands became clearer. General Motors, which had earned profits of $37.6 billion during its past 19 years, had vast resources to draw upon to finance whatever it wanted including a $30 billion-plus new car program for the 1979-1984 period — not to mention a cash flow from its sales. Ford Motor, despite its downturn in North America in the face of an ambitious $23 billion new product program, and some $13.8 billion in earnings since 1960, had its lucrative international operations to back up investments at home. Chrysler, in contrast, had sold most of its valuable assets abroad and at home, and by the end of 1978 was still in a scramble to raise the $7.5 billion it planned to spend between 1979 and 1984 to improve its products and competitive position. It was almost twice the amount that Chrysler had spent in the previous five years. With sales sagging, losses in the previous 19 years (1978 included) totaling $524 million over the same period, and profits since 1960 of only $2.6 billion, any fifth grader could tell that Chrysler was headed for tough sledding. The bottom line was simple: nothing must go wrong in the 1979 model year.

Long before the sense of financial troubles began to brew, the 1979 model year had been pegged by Ford Motor and Chrysler as a very special one. Both companies planned to introduce new, scaled-down full-size passenger cars and to test their competitive abilities against General Motors, which had already begun downsizing several of its car lines. Ford also had a sporty new subcompact Mustang to replace its original Mustang, a low-priced car that was a darling of the sporty market during the 1970's. Extra efforts were made by both companies to make their introductions for the 1979 model year more than the traditional multi-million dollar media razzmatazz to which the public had been subjected yearly at new car model time for decades.

Ford Motor chose to kick off its series by introducing the Mustang in July, 1978, giving its full-size cars the opportunity to gather public exposure separately at the traditional fall introductions. In its preparation for the two days of celebration at the Hyatt Regency Hotel in Dearborn, Michigan, across the road from Ford Motor's World Headquarters, Ford Motor press aides circulated thousands of press kits that included spicy quotes from Ford Motor president Lee Iacocca, along with a half-dozen or so photographs of Iacocca smiling ear-to-ear as he proudly stood next to his jewel of a new car. The momentum for a perfect introduction was at hand.

Suddenly, there was a major upset. Iacocca was abruptly fired only several days before the official press preview. He had been on the outs for several years with Henry Ford II, Ford Motor chairman. The two had clashed over future product policies with Iacocca apparently wanting to shift to smaller cars more quickly than Ford. It was the major bone of contention between them. In keeping with his style of acting in his own time, Ford lowered the boom.

The surprise timing of Iacocca's dismissal had Ford Motor press aides scrambling about the Detroit area, aggressively retrieving the press kits with Iacocca quotes and pictures. They were more than happy to replace them with new press kits containing spicy quotes from Ford Motor executive vice president William O. Bourke, along with a half dozen or so pictures of Bourke smiling ear-to-ear as he proudly stood next to his jewel of a new car.

The Iacocca firing turned into one of the hottest personnel stories of the auto industry in years and dashed any hopes that the company may have had for a smooth introduction of its new Mustang. For reporters, the essence of the occasion was best characterized by

Bourke when asked how he interpreted the Iacocca firing. "Some people throw firecrackers," the hard-nosed but cordial Bourke replied. "Others drop atomic bombs."

Chrysler also wasted no time in embarrassing itself while launching its 1979 models. It was a double dip, since the company had tripped badly earlier that year at its Warren, Michigan, tank plant. There, in February, 1978, Chrysler, the nation's only manufacturer of military battle tanks for the government, unveiled the XM-1, the Army's first battle tank in 19 years. As throngs watched, the 59-ton tank began demonstrating its versatility in a show that featured an unexpected trick. It got stuck in reverse. By fall, Chrysler and the government had somewhat recovered from the widespread publicity that the tank demonstration generated. Company aides nailed down every detail for ceremonies at the Lynch Road plant in Detroit to unveil the new Chrysler New Yorker and St. Regis. On hand to drive the first and second cars off the assembly line of the plant, which had undergone a $57 million renovation and retooling, were Michigan Governor William Milliken and Detroit Mayor Coleman Young.

Amid broad smiles, rolling news cameras and flashing bulbs, Governor Milliken casually positioned himself inside the first car, shut its door and began to wave as he turned the ignition switch. The car would not start. He tried again, and again nothing happened — its battery was dead.

Chrysler's new full-size cars were already a month behind schedule for delivery to dealer showrooms, despite the blitz of media promotions announcing that the cars were "at your Chrysler dealer now." The disappointing launch was matched by disappointing sales.

As the 1979 calendar year began, overall sales of new cars continued their upward trend, despite the rapidly decreasing sales at Ford Motor and Chrysler, which prompted scattered plant shutdowns and layoffs by those two auto makers. But by springtime, a rapid series of events had capsized the entire market, plunging America into gas-tank hysteria once again. Detroit was in a panic.

The new problems were clearly traceable to another round of costly oil price increases by OPEC in the beginning of 1979. In addition, Iran, an OPEC member with long-standing ties with the American government, underwent a tumultuous revolution that forced its monarch, Shah Mohammed Reza Pahlavi, to flee his country on January 16. As the revoluton spread, the forces in support of Iran's conservative Islamic leader, Ayatollah Ruhollah Khomeini, grew, leading to the disruption of Iran's oil production and oil exports. It was not so much that Iran was a major supplier of oil to the United States, but rather that the fall of Iran permeated America with new fears of another embargo and again pinned America to the ground. At the time of the Shah's departure, Iran was supplying 8.7 percent of the U.S. oil imports. By February 11, 1979, Khomeini returned to Iran from exile, assumed its leadership, and turned his nation's face away from America.

At home, the continuous OPEC price increases caused gasoline prices to accelerate. Spot gasoline shortages emerged in a number of states at various times during the spring and summer of 1979, further fueling the overall panic. As newspapers, radio and television stations reported the interruption in oil shipments from Iran, consumer gasoline lines grew in California and in small cities such as Levittown, Pennsylvania, and the fact that gasoline prices were hitting 80 cents to 90 cents a gallon caused "gas guzzlers" to be dropped like hot potatoes.

By mid-year, it was obvious that the 1979 model year was a complete disaster, with only a few American vehicles generating any excitement. Detroit had been caught again without the small automobiles conservation advocates had been pushing for over a decade, and this time the industry's bosses were persuaded that the shift in demand was permanent.

The impact of the abrupt slump on Chrysler was outlined at its July 31, 1979, news conference at which it appealed for government aid. In the first six months of 1979, the company had a loss of $260.9 million, of which $207.1 million was incurred in the April to June period. In its inventory were 80,000 unsold automobiles worth about $700 million. These were almost evenly divided between cars and trucks, each equipped with eight-cylinder engines, enough of a reserve to last for 95 days based on Chrysler's daily selling averages by its dealers. Its passenger car sales were down more than 15 percent and its trucks sales were substantially worse. In the three-month period between April and June, for example, Chrysler sold only 2,345 trucks for conversion into recreation vehicles, compared to 28,500 trucks in the same period a year earlier. During the first two weeks of June, 1979, after which top officals stopped counting, Chrysler received orders for only 12 recreation vehicle conversions nationally.

With capital expenditures for changing to more fuel-efficient product programs already locked into place at a cost of about $100 million a month, Chrysler acknowledged that its balance sheet would only look worse in the coming months. In financial centers, analysts quickly forecasted that Chrysler would lose $1 billion in 1979.

The auto industry's sense that the 1979 model-year disaster was to cultivate permanent change was further added to by several other surprises in the marketplace.

The full-size Chevrolet, a standard in America for decades, had slumped so badly in sales that by mid-summer General Motors recorded a 121-day inventory of the car, as compared to a "normal" 60-day supply. Sales of such recession and gas-price-proof automobiles as the Cadillac were also faltering. The Cadillac Seville, itself a downsized car with superior fuel economy over its larger predecessors, had become a sales lemon; inventories were running at a 100-day supply. In Oakland County in Michigan, one of the wealthiest counties in the nation, the lot at Wilson Crissman Cadillac overflowed with unsold cars and the massive showroom windows flashed banners offering sharp discounts.

By fall, the situation had worsened. Sales continued to plunge as the 1980 model year cars and trucks made their way into showrooms. Dealers found themselves tryng to sell their glut of unsold 1979 models alongside the 1980 models, most of which were merely warmed-over 1979 models. Auto workers were laid off by the thousands by the start of production for the new model year, not just at Chrysler, but at General Motors and Ford Motor as well. Evidence of the workers' concern was underscored by a United Automobile Workers union decision to eliminate Chrysler as a possible target for its industry master contract, which expired in September, 1979, and a statement, after selection of General Motors as the target company, that the union wanted to negotiate a contract without having to strike. It was so done.

The July-through-September quarter, traditionally a weak one for the industry due to the heavy expense incurred in retooling the plants for the new models, was more of a disaster than anticipated. Chrysler reported a loss of $460.6 million, at the time the largest quarterly loss to date in American business history. General Motors, the strong and mighty of the industry, reported an operating loss of $100 million. Ford Motor reported a world wide profit of $103 millon, but the figures only masked the dismal results in North America. Soon after the results for the period were released by Ford Motor, an internal document for review by top-ranking Ford executives only stated that the company anticipated a loss of $1 billion on its North American Automotive Operations division in 1979 and a loss of an equal amount in 1980. It sounded like a Chrysler in the making.

The American industry would end the decade of the 1970's on a sour note. Its 1979 total pasenger car sales, including the combined sales in the United States of General Motors, Ford Motor, Chrysler, American Motors and Volkswagen of America was 8,336,773 units, 10 percent below the 1978 total and the worst sales year since 1975. Just as unsettling, however, was the fact that foreign cars, primarily Japanese makes such as Toyota, Datsun, Honda, Subaru, Mazda and Mitsubishi, had captured a record 21.5 percent of all passenger car sales in the United States with their sales of 2,284,500 units, a 15.4 percent gain over 1978.

Battered Detroit was stumbling into the crucial 1980's pointing its finger of blame in every direction it could — Washington, the Middle East, the Orient. Someone was responsible for the quagmire in which it found itself, but who?

Chapter 7

"When we sort it all out, in my mind, there should never be a guarantee that anyone is insulated from competition."
Thomas A. Murphy

During his reign at Chrysler, Riccardo made it a point to meet and greet the public via press conferences at least once every three months. The occasions were the release of the company's financial results for the previous business quarters. Whether he brought good news or bad, Riccardo would dance to the music, something his competitors never dared to do on such a regular basis. Much could be learned about the workings of the industry in general from these gatherings, although they tended to be weighted with belly-achings about government intervention in the affairs of a sovereign nation — the Detroit automobile industry. But on slow news days, Chrysler could more often than not be looked to for a decent story. Inquisitive reporters could even cull out a hot news item from Riccardo's statements.

As the men and women of the automotive press corps gathered in the Chrysler press room on July 31, 1979, however, the feeling was definitely that the day's news conference would be more than routine.

Following standard procedure, Chrysler issued its financial results early that morning. Amid the discussion of the company's disastrous second quarter results, the report made reference to the fact that it had entered into discussions with the Federal Government for some sort of financial aid. What whetted appetites, however, was a statement released in Washington by the United States Treasury to the same effect. It was unusual. Within a few hours Riccardo was to drop his own style of a Henry Ford II kind of bomb at the regular press conference. It stunned the audience. The naive to the most seasoned of the reportorial corps listened in disbelief, and the shockwaves chased around the globe within hours.

Riccardo pointed out that in 1979 and 1980 Chrysler was to spend over $1 billion annually on engineering, research and development and for retooling its plants. Over half that amount, he added, was being spent in order to meet government standards. He continued: "Basically, the approach that we're taking is that the way for Chrysler to get some offset to the — the competitive disadvantage that we're suffering as a result of government regulations is to help us in the area of tax relief... and in as much as we are unable to carry back these losses because we have utilized up all our tax carry-backs we would propose a tax bill that would allow Chrysler to get an accelerated tax credit for the years 1979 and 1980 amounting to one-half of the expenditures."

So confident was Riccardo in the impressions he had received from Washington during his several weeks of shuttling back and forth that he declared: "With all of these kinds of signs of support, we feel justified in working on the assumption that some form of relief will be granted, and we have no other assumptions that we will make nor do we believe that any other assumption need be made."

The groundwork had been laid, he felt, for smooth sailing through the often illusively calm waters of the Washington merry-go-round. As reporters scrambled at the conclusion of the Riccardo press briefing to inform the world of the advent of a crucial test of the status quo in America, one reporter joked that he could imagine the cover of the next issue of Time Magazine: Riccardo taking the place of former New York City Mayor Abraham Beame, who had asked the government in 1975 for $1 billion in Federal loan guarantees to help the city avert bankruptcy. *Time's* cover then depicted Beame as a pauper, holding a tin cup and saying: "Brother, Can You Spare a Billion?"

On the face of it, the government should have had no problem in rejecting Chrysler's bid for aid. The nation's reputation, it would be argued, was built on survival of the fittest. The favored treatment and consequent change in the nation's tax laws could not be slipped through Congress easily. In addition, it was simply too tough to justify aid of such magnitude to a private concern of such magnitude. Chrysler was the 10th largest industrial company in America in 1978, had nearly $7 billion in assets, was the third-largest automobile manufacturer in the nation and the owner of one of the top 10 consumer credit companies, the Chrysler Financial Corporation. Chrysler's factory workers, most of them members of the politically powerful United Automobile Workers union, were among the highest-paid workers in the nation. Although middle management had seen its earning potential shaken time and time again as the company traversed one fiscal crisis after another, Chrysler's top executives remained among the highest paid in the nation, held memberships in all the "right" organizations (such as prestigious country clubs in suburban Detroit and prominent business organizations in New York and Washington), maintained mansions in the suburbs and usually flew first class.

There were other reasons why aid to the Chrysler Corporation could be quickly rejected. A hard look at the company would show that, in contrast to General Motors and Ford Motor, Chrysler was basically a regional manufacturing company. While it had operations spread through eight states — Michigan, Alabama, Illinois, Missouri, Indiana, Ohio, New York, Delaware — and the Ontario Province in Canada, nearly half the people directly employed by Chrysler lived in Michigan, the majority of them in and around Detroit. The company's national presence was only by virtue of its network of more than 4,000 car and truck dealers scattered around the country.

On the other hand, there were some persuasive arguments for government aid to Chrysler. From a global perspective, could America, for the sake of preserving long-held principles, continue to buck the world trend of other governments playing more active roles in helping their industries grow and beat American industry? Aiding Chrysler might be interpreted by other American businesses, regardless of their size, that once they fall upon hard times they could go to the Federal Government for financial help. Yet letting it fail could cost the already hard-pressed U.S. Treasury over half-a-billion dollars in unemployment and welfare benefits to the hundreds of thousands of workers who might be thrown out of work for indefinite periods of time. Then too, there was a widespread feeling within the industry that Chrysler's loss would only strengthen the hand of General Motors in dictating how the industry, and thus the nation, would be run.

From a political perspective Detroit was still a bastion of wealth that supported Democratic and Republican causes nationally and was home of some of the most politically prominent names on the national scene — Max Fisher, Henry Ford II, Mayor Coleman Young, Douglas Fraser. Despite the regionalism of the company, Chrysler was still among the three largest employers in Detroit, the nation's sixth largest city. In 10 Detroit area plants, blacks made up 50 percent of the work force. The nation was already in a recession that was striking blacks hardest, and even a temporary total shutdown of Chrysler could be devastating. Although Chrysler's dealers numbered only 4,000 they were sizable employers in their own communities. Also in the equation were suppliers to Chrysler which brought the total worker exposure in the event of a Chrysler shutdown to 500,000 people.

Riccardo struck more than a note with his proposal; several chords would be more accurate. Aiding Chrysler at the point and time in American history at which the issue was brought to a head set the stage for a full-fledged debate over the direction in which the nation was heading with respect to long-held American philosophies in the midst of a changing world. No sooner had his press conference ended than the nation's opinion makers seized the issue with a zeal that had not been demonstrated since the days of Watergate in the early 1970's, when corruption in the highest levels of American Government led to the downfall of President Richard M. Nixon.

Every major newspaper in the nation raised a skeptical eye, and prominent news columnists and commentators were even more blunt. *The New York Times,* the nation's newspaper of record, concluded in an August 2 editorial:

"Federal help might be a sensible last resort. But every avenue for restructuring Chrysler should be thoroughly explored first. Bailing out failing companies is a route the British have pursued with disastrous results. It is not a path the United States needs to follow."

The Wall Street Journal, the nation's leading business daily, also cast a wary eye at the request for aid in an editorial on August 3:

"Chrysler Corp.'s request for $1 billion in advance federal tax credits to bail it out of its serious financial difficulties is not something we can support. As England and any number of other countries have learned, government subsidies to sick corporations become a never-ending business, eventually applying a crushing burden on taxpayers and economic efficiency. To maintain a healthy economy government must simply let companies adapt to their changing fortunes, cutting losses before they become unmanageable."

The *Journal* then softened its tone:

"We must quickly add a note of sympathy for Chrysler. No doubt its managers have made their share of mistakes, in a market place that punishes mistakes severely. But sociologically, it is one of our favorite corporations. By virtue of its position — a huge concern up against even more powerful competitors — it has attracted a scrappy brand of managers, willing even to take on politicians where more secure firms hunker down. And if it is forced to the wall, no small part of the reason lies in those (mostly losing) political battles. In important ways it will be the victim of the new anti-corporation politics."

The Los Angeles Times, in a Sunday editorial on August 5 urged that the government "think twice."

The Washington Post fell in line with an August 2 editorial:

"The conventional case for a bailout is to preserve jobs. Chrysler had some 150,000 employees in this country, and perhaps twice as many more jobs indirectly dependent upon it through its suppliers and dealers, but preserving jobs merely to preserve jobs is dangerous.

"The British economy is the outstanding example of that policy's costs in low productivity and lethargic management.

"A bailout might also be defended as a defense of competition. General Motors already sells six out of every 10 American-built automobiles and the decline of Chrysler would leave it more heavily dominant than ever within the American industry. But the foreign cars offer a stronger guarantee of future competition than a weak domestic company propped up by public subsidies.

But the *Post,* published at the doorstep of the nation's government, also clearly saw the handwriting on the wall:

"On one point, Chrysler is in luck. It brings its troubles to the White House at a moment when the tenant there is confronting both a difficult re-election campaign and a recession. He could use a few friends in the Upper Mid-West, and in the labor movement. After a diligent study of the financial accounts and meditation on the equities he's likely to support a bailout — and Congress, for similar reasons, is likely to agree. The bailout is bad in principle but it's probably inevitable."

The battle lines formed quickly around the Chrysler aid issue with coalitions of a highly unusual nature emerging. The most notable was that of Thomas A. Murphy, chairman of General Motors, and Ralph Nader, the auto safety advocate who had been considered the company's number one enemy since the private eye caper of the 1960's. Both opposed government aid to Chrysler on the ground that it rewarded failure and compromised the free enterprise system.

It was Murphy's comments in an exclusive interview with *The New York Times,* published on August 2, 1979, that fired the first salvo.

"When we sort it all out, in my mind, there should never be a guarantee that anyone is insulated from competition," Murphy said quite firmly. "Competition is inherent in our American system and competition is what got us where we are today. As I look at the picture, every one of us in our industry and in many other industries have been importantly impacted by Government regulation and it's going to be a burden. And I don't think it gives us any advantage and Chrysler a disadvantage because one is larger or smaller than the other. But there is a problem, and I think something should be done about the Government standards. I think we should address the whole problem of regulation, sort it out and make sure it gives all Americans, all of the competitors, a fair shake."

Photo by Ira Rosenberg, "The Detroit Free Press."

Douglas Fraser, the president of the United Automobile Workers union, emerged as the power in Washington on Chrysler's behalf as it waged its battle for Federal aid. Fraser, the first labor union official ever elected to the board of directors of a major American corporation, started work at Chrysler on its assembly lines in the 1930's.

In his most piercing strike at Chrysler, Murphy said: "In my judgement there's never been a business that was viable that ever lacked financing."

It was only a matter of days before one of the harshest responses to Murphy's comments would come. Douglas Fraser, who had risen through the union ranks in the Chrysler factories and become president of the United Auto Workers, labeled Murphy's comments irresponsible and called the auto maker chief "a horse's ass." General Motors had no comment.

Although a full-scale public debate over the future of Chrysler did not emerge until late in the summer of 1979, a gradually developing bailout campaign had been underway since the winter of 1978.

It was on February 1, 1978, that Riccardo visited Stuart E. Eizenstat, chief domestic advisor to President Carter. In that brief meeting, Riccardo explained that Chrysler's profit picture at that time may have looked impressive but that he saw considerable difficulties for the company over the long haul. He said that the company hoped to raise about $8.5 billion to update its products to be more competitive in the marketplace and meet Federal standards for fuel economy and emissions, but overall it did not look good. Chrysler had been trying to raise money internally, he told Eizenstat, citing the sale of some overseas assets as a starter. He concluded his discussions by requesting Administration support for his effort to obtain a two-year freeze, for Chrysler only, on auto emissions standards at the 1978 level. If granted, Riccardo explained, the company could improve its cash flow by $600 million to $800 million a year.

Eizenstat listened receptively to the proposal but suggested that Riccardo try to line up some legislative support for his efforts. Meanwhile, apparently at Eizenstat's suggestion, Riccardo visited W. Michael Blumenthal, then Secretary of the Treasury. It was a good move. Blumenthal had come to the administration from Detroit, where he had been head of the Bendix Corporation, a leading supplier of automotive components. Unlike many Washington regulators who had never been to Detroit before they began regulating it, Blumenthal knew of the problems first hand. He knew what making automobiles was about.

Although unable to make any commitment, Blumenthal expressed an interest in trying to help. He assigned a deputy, Robert Carswell, to study the financial situation at Chrysler.

At about the same time as the White House meeting, Chrysler applied for a $250 million loan guarantee from the government through the Farmers Home Administration. The funds borrowed would be used to build a new facility in Richmond, Indiana. The application did prompt some action. The Administration had the loan guarantee program reviewed and determined that no loan could be guaranteed for over $50 million. The Richmond project was killed, after which Chrysler reapplied for a $50 million loan guarantee to cover expansion of its Kokomo, Indiana transmission plant. But this bid, made to the Economic Development Administration, was also rejected.

By fall, Riccardo and his top advisors had given up on becoming exempt from the government auto emissions standards compliance timetable. After talking with a number of law makers, Riccardo recalled later, he was convinced Congress "was in no mood to do that. It would be a politically naive thing to do."

As Chrysler's financial condition gradually worsened during 1978, Riccardo again went to the White House late in the year seeking help. Subsequently the Treasury assigned a person in the Domestic Capital Finance section to keep track of Chrysler.

Meanwhile, in Highland Park, a Chrysler tax man named Edward Sigler had begun to make headway with an idea about asking the government for a special tax credit. The idea had been bounced around before by Sigler but rejected by his superiors as unthinkable. This time it seemed to make more sense as top management ran out of options.

On the labor front, contract negotiations with the Big Three automakers were coming in mid-July of 1979, and Riccardo sought to establish an early understanding with the United Auto Workers. In late winter, Riccardo called Fraser's office, saying that he wanted to outline "a serious, emerging problem."

The meeting consisted of Riccardo, Fraser and staff aides from the union's Washington office, including Howard Paster, the union's chief lobbyist. Riccardo told the group that 1979 appeared as bad, if not worse than 1978, and that he had intensified his efforts in Washington to obtain regulatory relief as a means of improving the company's cash position.

Fraser responded by telling Riccardo he was not enthusiastic about the regulatory relief idea. There were several reasons, a participant in the meeting recalled. "First the competition would not stand for it, and second, regulatory relief that would give Chrysler money would (only) allow it to continue to sell cars that weren't selling already." The union had supported the fuel economy laws back in 1975, Fraser is said to have reminded Riccardo. Riccardo also tested the Sigler tax proposal on Fraser. The union chief was cool to that suggestion too, saying he felt the signals from Washington on that idea would be negative. Fraser suggested that the union might be receptive to supporting a government investment in Chrysler through the purchase of stock.

By the spring of 1979, market conditions were worsening as a result of the gas tank hysteria precipitated by the fall of the Shah of Iran and the continuing economic slowdown. Suddenly Chrysler's sales income was literally drying up as fast as its fund raising sources. (The sale of overseas and non-automotive assets was complete, Volkswagen had firmly withdrawn any interest in a partnership of any kind, as had several other potential suitors, and "The phone just didn't ring,"

File Photo from the United Auto Workers

Marc Stepp, vice president of the U.A.W. and director of its Chrysler Department, lost his chance to lead the union in its 1979 contract bargaining with the auto industry. Instead, he was thrust into the tougher role of persuading his constituents to take monumental contract concessions to help save Chrysler.

Riccardo recalled later.) An internal forecast that 1979 losses would be limited to $250 million was discarded and an all-out effort for government aid was launched.

Riccardo contacted Fraser and his aides again soon after the first meeting for suggestions of whom he might contact to help open doors in Congress. He had decided to make a go for it with the Sigler tax proposal. Among the names suggested was Thomas Hale Boggs Jr., son of the late House Majority leader T. Hale Boggs and Representative Corrine C. Boggs, both Democrats from Louisiana. Boggs, a specialist in tax law had done some odd job work for Chrysler previously, but nothing compared to what he would be asked this time. Among the other names suggested was William Timmons, a veteran door-opener in Washington, mostly on the Republican side of the fence. Riccardo dispatched his chief staff operative, Wendell Larsen, a Chrysler vice president, and Paul Heinen, another vice president, to determine who would be best. As it turned out, both Boggs and Timmons were hired, with the Boggs law firm of Patton, Boggs, and Blow taking the leadership role.

An overall game plan was devised in relatively short order, one that the United Auto Workers continued to agree with in economic terms but not in form. Fraser and Marc Stepp, who by then also had risen through the union ranks at Chrysler and moved into the union hierarchy as vice president and director of the Chrysler Department, decided to not consider Chrysler as a strike target in the upcoming master contract talks with the Big Three. Chrysler had already started laying off its workers by the thousands and if there were a strike, no winner could emerge. Riccardo and his top lieutenants began quickly studying new ideas for cutting costs to preserve the increasingly endangered cash flow. Meanwhile in Washington, Chrysler's entire lobbying efforts were under the direction of Larsen, with the exception of the union effort. The Administration and all of Washington would be swept in an all-out effort to line up support. Riccardo himself would do the actual pitching, meeting as many as 10 lawmakers in a single day. Exhausted by night, he spent much of his evenings assessing progress, if any, and went back at it again by sunrise.

At the suggestion of Boggs and his associates, a tax proposal much like the one conceived by Sigler was presented to Senator Russell E. Long, another Louisiana Democrat who was chairman of the Senate Finance Committee, the committee that deals with taxes. Representative Al Ullman, chairman of the House Ways and Means Committee, was also solicited for his help and expressed his willingness to consider acting favorably on the measure if other support could be found. The campaign appeared to gather scattered support.

With a small contingent of senators from the Chrysler states, the Chrysler team approached Secretary Blumenthal. He embraced the idea, one of the Chrysler team members recalled, "said he thought it was reasonable." He sent the Chrysler representatives to his tax staff and back to Congress.

By mid-July, the wheels appeared well greased. Although Senator Long had no real interest in the future of Chrysler, he saw the tax credit campaign as a golden opportunity to further advance his populist form of Southern capitalism: employee stock ownership plans. If Chrysler would agree to further employee ownership in the company (already over 30 percent of its stock was owned by employees, one of the highest percentages of all the auto companies), Long would push the bill through his committee. Blumenthal saw it as an ideal opportunity to become a hero in Detroit and perhaps buttress his eroding power within the Administration. Riccardo and Fraser saw the effort by then as the only way to save Chrysler jobs. White House staffers, particularly Eizenstat, viewed a successful Congressional effort as a means of addressing the potential unemployment situation and winning points for President Carter, whose popularity in labor circles was crumbling under the increasing attractiveness of Senator Edward Kennedy as a presidential candidate.

The public announcement that Chrysler was discussing some sort of Federal aid served as the symbolic firing of the gun to begin the race. No sooner had the tax prosposal idea been nailed down and the major forces in the Administration and Congress lined up that something of monumental consequence went wrong again. Chrysler, an innocent bystander, fell victim to the management shake-ups that are common to high government. Blumenthal, who had been squabbling with senior White House staff members over access to the President and his role in fiscal policy making, was forced to resign on July 19. The surprise development cast serious doubt on the future of the tax advance strategy. To compound Chrysler's troubles, the White House quickly announced that Blumenthal would be replaced by G. William Miller, then chairman of the Federal Reserve Board and the former chairman at Textron.

Miller was no stranger to the Chrysler situation. In the course of keeping various agency heads apprised of the company's fluid situation and its plans to strengthen its fiscal position, Riccardo had visited Miller on several occasions. In those meetings, Riccardo learned that Miller was unalterably opposed to the tax credit idea. Instead, he suggested, Chrysler should consider selling off even more of its assets or try the bankruptcy route. When the White House announced Miller's new job, every heart in Chrysler senior management skipped a beat. A friend had been replaced with an adversary, and that was the last thing the company needed.

Despite the political setback, Riccardo and his campaign strategists concluded that there was still sufficient interest in Washington to aid the company and that an outside chance existed in getting the tax bill through in spite of Miller. He was a strong player in the Administration but not the only player. And the forces in Congress, such as Senator Long, flexed considerable muscle themselves when they got behind an idea. There was the less complicated reason also; Chrysler had no alternative but to press ahead, having rejected bankruptcy and scaled down as much as it thought it could.

One of Miller's first actions after being sworn into office was to state at an August 9 press conference his strong opposition to the Chrysler tax plan. He had persuaded the White House to conduct further studies of Chrysler's request along the lines of a possible loan guarantee plan providing for considerably less than the company sought. Miller was thinking of a figure in the neighborhood of $500 million — $750 million tops. Not only had the tables been turned on Chrysler and the United Auto Workers with respect to the form aid from Washington might take and the amount they could expect, but also the players involved in the decision-making process continued to change radically.

Chrysler's plan for survival had slipped from the hands of Senator Long and Representative Ullman, by then considered friends of Chrysler's proposed legislation. It landed on the doorsteps of Senator William Proxmire, a Wisconsin Democrat and chairman of the Senate Banking Committee, and Representative Henry S. Reuss, another Wisconsin Democrat and chairman of the House Banking Committee. Both lawmakers were cool to the idea of loan guarantees.

Neither Proxmire or Reuss were strangers to special tax legislation. In 1967, they marshaled through a key provision in the present tax code that increased the time period in which losses could be applied against reported earnings from three years to five years. The beneficiary was the American Motors Corporation, Wisconsin's largest private employer. With adoption of the legislation, American Motors was allowed to take a tax loss credit of $19 million and apply it to the first fiscal quarter of 1968. But since then, Proxmire had led the opposition to and voted against two key loan guarantee measures — the $250-million loan guarantee program in 1971 for the Lockheed Aircraft Corporation and, in 1975, a $2.3-billion loan program for New York City. Reuss also voted against the Lockheed loan guarantee program, although he was in favor of the loan plan for New York City.

By mid-August, Chrysler was again rewriting its entire bailout proposal. It was under orders from Miller to come up with more details regarding the company's efforts to salvage itself. Congress was recessed, and the next move did not take place until after Labor Day, 1979. By then Chrysler's financial situation had eroded further, and its sudden and accelerated borrowing of funds from a revolving loan agreement with a group of banks prompted the banks to place a freeze on future borrowings. Chrysler's Japanese trade partner, Mitsubishi, meanwhile, began seeking ways out of its long-term small car distribution arrangement. To further save its dwindling cash supplies, Chrysler initiated a round of white-collar layoffs numbering 5,000 people, striking yet another blow at the sinking morale of Chrysler workers. The company's two top executives were to take a pay cut to $1 a year from their previous salaries of $360,000 a year, and to work for credits whose value would be tied to the value of company stock. But morale sank again with the imposition of pay cuts ranging from 2 percent to 5 percent for 1,700 management workers who were spared the ax. They also agreed to work for credits.

Amid the near chaotic atmosphere, special interest groups had found the Chrysler crisis an opportunity to advance some ideas that had been frustrated for lack of a proper arena.

Senator Long, for example, found Chrysler's problems as the best platform yet to push his stock ownership philosophy. Likewise, General Motors and the United Auto Workers found some good in Chrysler's hard times.

Despite chairman Murphy's personal feelings about government rescues of failing businesses, there was no real desire on the part of General Motors for Chrysler to fail. The anti-trust question was of some concern. More important, however, after years of complaining, in a relatively low profile position in comparison with Chrysler, about the evils of government regulation, General Motors raised the Chrysler situation as an example of what could happen to an essential industry when the government seeks to regulate it. By citing the ills that helped create the need for a Chrysler bailout, General Motors certainly looked down the road for an easing of regulations for the entire industry. In that manner it could achieve in Washington, through Chrysler, something it was never able to accomplish on its own. If Chrysler could save millions of dollars by virtue of the government relaxing some standards here or there, General Motors could save hundreds of millions.

Fraser and his associates at the union were not asleep at the switch either. Since its last round of master contract talks in 1976, Fraser had been pushing for labor representation on the boards of directors of the various automakers. At Chrysler, where he was then chief union negotiator, management rejected the demand out of hand even though the company was familiar with such input into corporate policy making by virtue of its operations in Europe. Labor representatives sat on boards of several European automakers in which the Americans had substantial interest. Chrysler's anticipated appeal in 1979 to the union to make unprecedented major contract concessions in wages and benefits posed the perfect opportunity to force union representation. The union would be hard pressed to strike the company if that battle was lost, yet Chrysler management also knew that the last thing it could tolerate in 1979 was a strike.

For Coleman A. Young, the politically tough and savvy mayor of Detroit, the Chrysler crisis also presented an opportunity. Young was an early supporter of President

Carter in 1976 when Jimmy Carter was casting about the nation in search of people who would recognize him as a viable presidential candidate. In exchange for Young's political support, Carter later did what he could to channel Federal money into the cities, particularly Detroit, to help urban areas rebuild their socio-economic bases. Carter had paid his political debts long before the Chrysler situation crystallized. But Young reminded the White House that, as a friend and one who intended to continue to support Carter in 1980, he felt Chrysler required immediate attention.

For the Chrysler board, the crisis meant a chance to install new blood at the top. For all the good Chrysler's top managers may have been able to do for their company, the low points of their tenure always overshadowed their highs. Such was the case with Keller, Colbert, Townsend and, in 1979, with Riccardo in the face of the Chrysler collapse. As public debate on the issue expanded, a growing school of thought emerged that a prerequisite to salvation was the cleansing of Chrysler's corporate soul. Many felt that Riccardo, the man who scaled Chrysler down in order to keep the company breathing as long as it had but who was reluctant to hurriedly downsize his products to meet fuel economy standards, had to go. It came as no surprise to Riccardo that public sentiment was swinging in that direction. Even he had recognized a need for change in the front office long before his bailout appeal.

Riccardo's elevation in October, 1975, to chairman and chief executive officer of Chrysler had not taken place with the full and enthusiastic support of the company's board of directors. Although Riccardo seemed the logical choice to succeed Townsend after having served as president for nearly five years, some board members were uncomfortable with him and had decided that he was too abrasive. These members had their eyes set on another board member, Eugene A. Cafiero, then the executive vice president of the company. Cafiero, who was promoted to president when Riccardo was made chairman, joined the Chrysler payroll in 1953 when Chrysler purchased the Briggs Manufacturing Company, the maker of bodies for all Chrysler cars. Cafiero had worked his way up the ladder at Chrysler, and his supporters felt he was as qualified as Riccardo to handle the top spot. When the succession deal was finally cut, however, the Chrysler board chose to have a top management team similar to that at General Motors, with a finance man at the top, Riccardo, and an engineering man, Cafiero, as president and chief operating officer, keeping the shop running and welded together.

Riccardo and Cafiero saw Chrysler's future in different perspectives and during their tenure together that compounded the company's problems. Riccardo was a pessimist. He saw the problems facing the company as being much more serious than did Cafiero, and unlike Cafiero he didn't see where the money Chrysler needed was coming from. Cafiero, an optimist, felt the needed funds could be raised through increased sales of the company's new models. But as the scramble for money progressed, the manufacturing side of the company reflected the problems as new product launches fell behind schedule, and decisions by committees were often slow in coming or never made. Also, the new car models did not blaze the trails hoped for. Riccardo gained credibility with his directors, although the company's reputation was taking a beating. In November, 1978, Cafiero was forced to resign as president and assumed the position of vice chairman, a new post, for a brief period.

Lee Iacocca, the ousted president of Ford Motor, was named president of Chrysler. The news was stunning. The master salesman of the American automobile business, demoted and assigned to an isolated Ford Motor warehouse all in a matter of a few weeks, had decided to stage a comeback by tackling the toughest job in the industry — saving the Chrysler Corporation. His appointment

Photo by John Collier, "The Detroit Free Press."

Lee Iacocca had hoped to someday be head of the Ford Motor Company. But the master salesman of the American automobile industry was abruptly fired from the presidency of Ford Motor in the summer of 1978, ending years of feuding between he and Henry Ford 2nd, chairman of Ford Motor. Iacocca left Ford Motor a few months later to become president of the Chrysler Corporation where he was charged with delivering the struggling automaker from disaster.

was announced by *The Wall Street Journal,* which carried a detailed account of the terms under which Iacocca was to be hired and the price Chrysler was paying to land the tough-talking Mr. Magic of the automobile business, the man with the reputation for selling the sizzle as well as the steak. Once on board, Iacocca joined forces with an old friend, Harold Sperlich, whom Riccardo had hired away from Ford Motor a few years earlier to design Chrysler's new cars for the 1980's.

Iacocca did not come cheap. He accepted a base salary of $360,000, the same as Riccardo, although considerably less than what he made at Ford Motor. Chrysler was to pay him an additional $1.5 million in installments between January 2, 1979, and June 30, 1980, most of that reimbursement for severance money Iacocca lost by breaking the terms of his separation agreement from Ford Motor, which had stipulated that he not work for a competitor for at least two years. Chrysler also gave him an option to purchase 400,000 shares of stock in the company. Just as important, however, Riccardo promised Iacocca in a letter dated October 26, 1978, that he would recommend that Iacocca be named chief executive officer of the company in January, 1980. Riccardo, who would then be only 55 years old, had decided to bite the bullet. He would remain as chairman but would cede full control of the company to Iacocca.

Riccardo had earlier tried to shake someone loose from General Motors but no one would talk to him. He could not get inside the channels of trivia to even learn who might be available. But the Iacocca catch was as impressive as any that might have been landed from General Motors. At a news conference on November 2, 1978, officially introducing Iacocca as company president, Riccardo told reporters the choice was made because he needed more "firepower" at the top levels of the company. He got it.

Iacocca, a tall, sharp-tongued man whose trademarks were dark blue, pin-striped suits and Havana cigars "sent from friends," was once described as being "worth his weight in gold," by Robert S. McNamara, one of the Ford Motor Whiz kids who eventually rose to the company presidency. It was a tribute to the salesmanship abilities of the Allentown, Pennsylvania, native, who was discovered in 1956 from among the masses of Ford Motor's district sales managers as a result of a clever sales slogan he dreamed up to help spark slumping sales in his Washington, D.C. district. It was simple: "56 for 56" . Specifically, a new Ford car could be purchased in 1956 for $56 a month. The gimmick catapulted Iacocca's district from 32nd, near the bottom, to first place in sales, and Iacocca to Ford's headquarters in Dearborn. Once there, he took on any challenge thrust before him and any opponent who might block his path to his ultimate goal of meriting Henry Ford II's blessings to succeed him as head of the company. It was his zeal for that spot and willingness to challenge Ford himself on key product policy decisions that led to Iacocca's ouster.

The significance of Iacocca's move to Chrysler cannot be overstated. Not since Walter Chrysler, one of the most distinguished executives in the automobile business in his time, came out from retirement to oversee the reorganization of Maxwell-Chalmers, had anyone of such prestige in the industry risked his reputation by joining the ranks of a failing automaker with a pledge to turn it around. If Riccardo needed to sell someone in Washington or anywhere else on his determination to bring top rank talent to the company to help steer it through the choppy waters ahead, he had only to inform them that his successor would be Lee Iacocca. He was, as one Chrysler executive put it, "the epitome of confidence."

Not long after Iacocca came on board, the revolving doors of Chrysler and Ford Motor began spinning as resignations flew and heads rolled. The shaping of the "Iacocca Motor Company" was about to begin. He dragged two former Ford Motor executives out of retirement: J. Paul Bergmoser, a specialist in purchasing, and Gar Laux, a specialist in sales. He persuaded Gerald Greenwald, a 22-year veteran at Ford who was president of Ford of Venezuela, to join Chrysler as its controller.

By late summer of 1979, when even Iacocca realized that the company was in much worse shape than he had thought, puzzled onlookers were asking why these people dared gamble their reputations on Chrysler. Bergmoser would declare: "I have faith in Lee's leadership." Laux, while horrified by the condition of the sales organization and dealer network, would voice also his confidence in Iacocca's abilities to take on the tough challenge: "It's a rewarding experience to work with a guy like Lee." Greenwald would offer a similar reason.

In contrast to their past work experiences with Iacocca, however, they faced the reality that in the past he made good with a company that made good. This time, at perhaps the most crucial juncture in his life, Iacocca was trying to make a comeback with a company that was attempting the same. And he had the whole job thrust into his lap much sooner than anticipated. On September 18, 1979, Riccardo retired.

Earlier that spring, Riccardo had been rushed to a hospital with cardiac trouble, missing a trip to Washington where he would have had an opportunity to consult with President Carter during a White House summit meeting of automobile executives and Cabinet members assembled to address the emerging problems of the industry. Riccardo's physician released him with orders to retire immediately or run the risk of killing himself in the near future from exhaustion. After a few weeks at home, where strategy meetings were held, Riccardo was again back on the street soliciting help and support wherever he could find it, a process that shifted into even higher gear after his July press conference.

In his letter announcing his retirement, Riccardo wrote: "Even though I have actively addressed the major problems facing Chrysler, in the minds of many I am closely associated with the past management of a troubled company." Referring to his hospital stay in the spring and his physician's advice, he added, "I felt at the time that, in view of Chrysler's situation, I should stay on until the end of the year in order to provide the funds necessary to return Chrysler to profitability. A large part of that effort has now been completed. Even though the final amount is not yet fixed, the Administration has agreed that it will support a Federal loan guarantee... I am confident, therefore, that the necessary assistance will be provided. It would be most unfair to the new management and to the employees of Chrysler if my continued presence as board chairman should in any way hinder the final passage of our requests for Federal loan guarantees."

Riccardo, saying that he felt the time was "appropriate" for him to heed his physician's advice, surrendered his post of chief executive officer and chairman, both of which went to Iacocca, and resigned from the company's board of directors.

Riccardo's departure did much to improve Chrysler's image in Washington, which perceived Chrysler as a failing company in the hands of incompetents. But while Iacocca's presence spoke highly of the caliber of new management, it did little to change the thinking about whether the company should get Federal aid. The new chief did not help matters any during his early days of leadership by blaming the government for many of the company's misfortunes. It was a stance Iacocca had brought with him from Ford Motor, and one he had to tone down if Chrysler was to get sympathy in Washington.

"From the beginning, we argued that the Goverment got us into the soup and it ought to help us get out," Larsen recalled. "We used that pitch until the Congressional hearings started and then after that we used it less and less because it worked less and less."

That the big-Government-bad-guy argument poisoned the waters was hammered home by James Blanchard, a young Democrat in the House of Representatives whose district just north of Detroit, in Oakland County, was a cross between blue collar and white-collar workers on all levels, most of them involved in the automobile industry, many of them employed at Chrysler. Blanchard, an early supporter of Chrysler's efforts and the man who marshaled efforts on the company's behalf in the House, had been testing the waters to determine the sentiment of his fellow lawmakers toward helping the company. An overwhelming majority told him point blank that they had no interest in saving Chrysler. Saving the jobs of the workers, on the other hand, was a totally different issue. With that bit of insight, the strategy changed dramatically. The hard-nosed business types retrenched, yielding the floor to Fraser and the auto workers.

If there was an organization that understood the mystiques of both Detroit and Washington, it was the United Auto Workers. Far from burning its bridges in the years of dealing in Washington as some company bosses had, the union had cultivated an intimate relationship with the government and had developed an ability to influence thinking in Washington as in Detroit. The Chrysler issue was a natural since the union's vested interest could not be closer to home; the union had some 123,00 members whose jobs were at stake.

Fraser and the union suddenly occupied a pivotal position in several respects. The union had a contract to negotiate with Chrysler and it was certain that the outcome of those talks would influence the thinking of many members of Congress and key Administration players such as Secretary Miller, who was beating the drums after Labor Day for more of a sacrifice on Chrysler's part. By the same token, it was well understood in the Administration that President Carter's popularity with Fraser had taken a decided turn downwards in the face of the nation's worsening economic woes and spreading unemployment. Fraser also had spearheaded a new political movement called the Progressive Alliance. Although it did not endorse candidates, the alliance was a forum for constant criticism of Carter's social policies. Meanwhile, Fraser was beginning to warm to the idea of backing Senator Edward Kennedy in the 1980 presidential primaries, due to start in a matter of weeks after the Congressional hearings began.

Fraser led the campaign to drive home the human suffering that would take place if Chrysler was allowed to fail. This was the basis of his argument for Federal aid from the start, but Fraser's position was often overshadowed by Chrysler front office declarations, which tended to draw more attention. Blanchard and the Chrysler supporters in Congress had new ammunition as Chrysler began to crank out detailed documents on its operations with such information as the number of employees it had in every Congressional district in the nation, plus the numbers working for Chrysler suppliers and where those companies were located. In the Administration, where even President Carter initially had frowned on the idea of a Chrysler bailout, Eizenstat, who understood economics and unemployment, was impressed by the new arguments. Likewise impressed was Vice President Walter Mondale, an old friend of Fraser's from Mondale's days as a senator from Minnesota. The Vice President was apprised of Chrysler's needs first-hand in early September in Detroit thanks to Larsen, who attended a luncheon they were both invited to and managed to sit next to Mondale during the meal. Afterwards, they spent nearly half-an-hour together before Mondale returned to Washington with some fresh thinking on the subject.

The new thrust was working, but nothing firm happened in Washington until the United Auto Workers set a contract with Chrysler on October 25. (It was nearly six weeks after the old contract with the company had expired, yet workers stayed on their jobs.) On all counts, it was a pain and suffering contract. The union broke Big Three bargaining tradition and gave Chrysler major concessions that added up to approximately $203 million in breaks from the contract already accepted by General Motors and Ford Motor. These concessions were in addition to some $100 million in deferred payments to the pension fund, which was already running a $1 billion deficit.

The new pact also called for Fraser to be nominated by Iacocca for a seat on the Chrysler board, a first in American industry.

In announcing the new pact with Chrysler, Fraser told reporters: "These actions make it clear that the U.A.W. has met its responsiblities in the broad effort to save Chrysler workers' jobs and restore the company to stability. The burden now rests on the Congress to act promptly to assist Chrysler as well as on the banks, supplier companies and others with a stake in this matter."

The agreement was announced a day after a breakfast meeting in Washington at the home of Vice President Mondale, one of several that the Vice President held in an attempt to keep the lines of communications open between the union and the Administration. Attending the breakfast, in addition to Fraser were Stepp, Miller and Eizenstat. Miller's attitude at the session struck Fraser and his associates the wrong way; the emphasis Miller placed upon the President's upcoming bid for re-election prompted Mondale to politely suggest that the statements be disregarded. A Fraser aide suggested that Miller "be exposed." "We could have destroyed this guy if we went out and repeated what he said," the aide told Fraser. But the union boss ignored both and dealt with Mondale.

Selling Chrysler workers on the concessions in the contract was a tough proposition, recalled Charles Williams, president of Chrysler Local 110 in Warren,

Michigan. Workers at the Warren Truck plant had spent about as much time laid off as they had worked in that year and were in no mood to talk about more concessions, Williams said. "But everybody realized after a while that the company wasn't trying to fool us this time. It was really in trouble." With only minor dissension, the 256-member Chrysler Bargaining Council approved the pact on October 31, virtually assuring approval by the rank and file. Fraser and Stepp did not hear the final vote by the council, which convened for a two-day session in Kansas City, Missouri, on October 31. In an unusual development, they had left abruptly for Washington at the request of Vice President Mondale, who persuaded Fraser and Stepp of the "urgency" of a meeting to be held on the Chrysler aid situation. Mondale had made it a point while pushing the Chrysler efforts in the Administration to include Fraser in the discussions. A plane was chartered and upon their arrival in Washington they were given priority clearance at the National Airport. Something big had been going on in Washington besides the annual trick or treat feats for Halloween night. Indeed there had.

The Administration, after rejecting two previous Chrysler proposals, had finally drawn up a plan with which it could live. To the surprise of all, President Carter had decided to ask Congress to approve a $1.5 billion loan guarantee program for ailing Chrysler. It was twice the amount Miller had been saying the Administration could ever imagine supporting and was far in excess of what Chrysler itself had initially sought. Fraser and his cohorts were elated, and left immediately for Kansas City to rejoin their fellow workers and spread the good news.

In explaining the drastic change of position, Secretary Miller later told reporters that there had been a "change in outlook" for the auto industry and the general economy. "It is apparent to us that any financial assistance plan should be adequate and sufficient to accomplish the purpose," Miller declared. He went on to elaborate on the human pain and suffering and the adverse impact on communities across the nation if Chrysler was allowed to fail. The only catch to the whole proposal was that Chrysler would have to raise new commitments to help itself by an additional $1.5 billion. In effect, Chrysler would get a $3 billion refinancing.

With the Administration finally committed to a firm figure and the terms set, Congress was ready to stage a free-for-all debate over the merits of the biggest corporate bailout in the nation's history.

After nearly three months of intensified lobbying, the various Chrysler campaign teams had concluded that their chances of getting a Chrysler bill through the House looked relatively good. A fair number of its members were sympathetic to labor, and a good number who had no direct Chrysler constituency and thus did not care which way the vote went would probably go with the measure since it would not hurt their standing with the leadership. House Speaker Thomas O'Neill appeared to take a special interest in the Chrysler measure, setting up a 35-member leadership task force to help marshal the activities at the suggestion of Federal lawmakers from the Northeast and Midwest. On the Senate side, the ball playing was tougher; there was not the same cry of human suffering and emotionalism as was heard in the House.

The first round of House action came swiftly with the November 15 approval by the House Banking Committee of the Administration's loan guarantee bill. The vote was 25 to 17. The measure provided for $1.5 billion in loan guarantees over a 10-year period, providing the company raised another $1.5 billion from its suppliers, lenders, dealers, employees and state and local governments.

The Senate was much tougher, however. With Senator Proxmire garnering considerable support from conservative Republicans, a compromise plan to provide Chrysler with $4 billion in new money was adopted on November

29 — but it asked a lot more of everyone involved. The measure was contingent upon Chrysler workers accepting a three-year wage freeze worth $1.32 billion. Despite objections from a small minority on the committee that the measure, as proposed, would make paupers of the workers while keeping the company alive, it was adopted 10 to 4. The measure also raised the ante to be asked for from the suppliers, creditors and dealers. Fraser rejected the proposal, telling the Senate committee on November 19 that his colleagues had made "a sufficient sacrifice." Despite his appeals, the tough changes in the loan guarantee measure were left intact by another banking committee vote of 10 to 5.

The Senate bill differed from that of the Administration and the House Banking Committee in several key respects, the most significant being the raise in workers' contributions. (The Administration considered the $203 million concession already made by the union as sufficient.) The tough wage concessions were the idea of Paul Tsongas, a freshman Democrat from Massachusetts, and Richard Lugar, a freshman Republican from Indiana. A former mayor of Indianapolis, Lugar rose to national prominence during the debate over a Federal loan guarantee for New York City. A tough critic of that aid proposal, Lugar dropped his opposition after more stringent provisions were written into the bill.

The rationale behind the wage freeze in the Chrysler pact, Lugar and Tsongas explained, was to insure the company's survival and to discourage other companies from seeking Federal bailouts. Fraser said he was always puzzled that such a move to penalize the company would be aimed straight at the hearts of workers.

As the Chrysler aid bill began making its way to the final legislative stages, the Chrysler campaign team launched its last round of efforts to line up support. The company sent out a call to its dealers, asking them to come to Washington at their own expense and spend a few days visiting members of Congress and others involved with the bailout effort. It was one of the best-organized campaigns to sweep Washington in some time.

"In the process we had 1,700 dealers, and not all of them were Chrysler dealers," recalled Dois Rosser, owner of Poquoson Motors in Hampton, Virginia. Rosser, a self-proclaimed conservative wasn't too keen on the idea of the bailout except that he too felt the government should share some responsiblity for his company's ills. He joined Bryan Wilkinson, from Murray, Utah, Bill Kline from Covington, Kentucky, (who thought his congressman would never see him) and Lou Casing from Pittsburgh, Pennsylvania. Jack Hefley, owner of River Oaks Chrysler in Houston, sent his general sales manager up for a full week to help make the rounds. The dealers were mostly Republican, mostly consevative and more often than not contributors to the campaigns of the lawmakers in office. They were a natural for this job.

Under the supervision of Chrysler's Larsen, the dealers were to fan out in groups of 10 seeking an audience with whomever would speak to them. Their assignment was to determine where each member of Congress stood on the emerging Senate version of the Chrysler aid bill, report their findings and, in the case of a negative position, determine what could be done to change it. Hardly a soul with a vested interest in the outcome of the Chrysler legislation was missed. Even Congress Watch, the consumer advocate agency sparked by Ralph Nader, which opposed aid to Chrysler, was approached. Escorting that group was Jerry Pyle, a Chrysler vice president. After hearing the group's pitch, Howard Symons, staff attorney for Congress Watch, spoke admiringly of the effort. "It's much easier to vote against a corporation or Lee Iacocca than a guy who lives in your district," Symons said. "Their argument was that Chrysler was ready to go with its new cars, it could do a good job, that if they don't get the money a lot of dealers would go out of business. You couldn't walk the corridor of any official building without seeing a group of dealers huddled deciding who to meet with next," Symons added.

"I believe I changed some minds," declared Bryan Wilkinson after the loan guarantee bill was passed. "I'm a very conservative, Mormon Republican and I studied this hard. But what is the government for if not to provide a service?" Wilkinson, owner of Cottonwood Chrysler Plymouth in Utah hustled Senator Jake Garn, the ranking Republican on the Senate Banking Committee, who, like Senator Proxmire, committee chairman, was opposed to the Chrysler loan guarantee bill. "Garn did one thing he promised, he'd do," said Wilkinson. "He did promise that he would get the bill out of committee so that it could have a full airing on the Senate floor. Without his help, I don't think the bill would have gotten to the floor," said Wilkinson who campaigned in 1980 for Garn's reelection to the Senate. In total, Wilkinson spent nearly a month in Washington campaigning for Chrysler.

Final action on the Chrysler bill did not come until the last week of the Congressional session before the Christmas break. It was a scary situation, for Chrysler officials had said that without action before the start of 1980 the company would simply not be able to raise or generate enough money to carry it through until Congress reconvened.

It was clear from the start that if problems arose they would be in the Senate. When the House began its deliberatons on December 18, it was almost a foregone conclusion that it would act affirmatively.

There were a number of last-minute manuevers on the House floor to take more out of the hides of the workers, and the worker concessions eventually were raised to $400 million from the $203 million in the original bill, with the employee stock ownership plan raised to $150 million. But after lengthy debate, the icing was put on the cake in the House by Speaker O'Neill, who gave a rare, emotion-packed speech to his fellow lawmakers on the need to adopt the Chrysler bill. "I don't think we can afford not to take the chance," O'Neil declared. "Laying off 700,000 people, you'll start a chain reaction. And we won't be able to dig ourselves out for 10 years." The House approved the Chrysler loan guarantee bill by a vote of 271 to 136.

In the Senate, worker pay was again at the heart of the debate. Three senators, Thomas Eagleton of Missouri, William Roth of Delaware and Joseph Biden of Delaware, had proposed a substitute bill to replace the one adopted earlier by the Senate Banking Committee. The difference was that the Eagleton-Roth Amendment, as it was called, lowered the worker sacrifice to $400 million from the $1.32 billion proposed by the banking committee bill. Lugar insisted on an $800 million compromise if one had to be accepted at all. The United Auto Workers already had served notice that it did not feel it could get its members to swallow a three-year wage freeze, and thus the entire effort would be washed away — along with Chrysler — unless a compromise could be found.

The pro-Chrysler forces did not have enough votes to beat Lugar and a meeting was quickly held in the office of Senator Donald Riegle, Democrat from Michigan, who was among those heading the Chrysler effort in the Senate. A head count revealed that the group did not even have 40 votes. An all-out, last-ditch effort was launched to convince senators to vote in favor of the Eagleton-Roth measure. Responsiblities were divided up and in two hours the union had picked up 15 votes. The Eagleton-Roth Amendment was approved by the Senate by a vote of 54 to 43. Action on the final bill was jeopardized, however, by Senator Lowell P. Weicker, a liberal Republican from Connecticut, who again pressed the wage concession question. The same forces that had earlier gone through one battle again agreed to a compromise, requiring a union concession of $462.2 million. The compromise was accepted, and the Senate approved the Chrysler Loan Guarantee Act of 1979 on December 19, by a vote of 53 to 44. On December 20 and December 21, the House and Senate took final actions on the Chrysler aid pact and sent it to President Carter for his signature.

Chrysler, with its hurriedly assembled but well-knit human agony campaign, had done in a matter of weeks what normally might have taken several years to achieve. Merry Christmas, Washington would say to Detroit. It was a desperately needed gift.

Chapter 8

"The final chapter hasn't been written yet."

David W. Knapp

President Carter signed the Chrysler Corporation Loan Guarantee Act of 1979 into law on January 7, 1980. Soon thereafter, the Chrysler media magicians, Kenyon & Eckhardt, the agency that had handled Ford Motor advertising for 34 years until Iacocca persuaded them to join him at Chrysler, began spending hundreds of thousands of dollars for mass media thank-you notes from "The New Chrysler Corporation." Indeed, there was something new about this old bastion of private enterprise. It had set the wheels in motion for the establishment of a major government-sponsored American automobile company whose policies and practices would hence be influenced even more by the very bureaucrats in Washington who for so long had been the enemy, and by the sweaty assembly lines. It was a deal Chrysler had not wanted, for more debt — of any kind — was the last thing the company needed. A tax plan would have been an asset on the books; the loans were liabilities. But it was the only deal in town.

Gaining access to the badly needed finances provided for in the loan guarantee legislation was no easy task, as Chrysler executives learned in the weeks to come. There were numerous hurdles that the old Chrysler Corporation had to first clear before it could drink from the government well. The law, which was administered by a Loan Guarantee Board, set specific targets for contributions from the various interests involved with Chrysler. It was a shopping list:

• Existing American lenders were required to extend $400 million in new credit and $100 million in concessions on existing loans.

• Foreign lenders were required to extend an additional $150 million credit to Chrysler.

• Chrysler had to sell enough assets to raise $300 million.

• Suppliers had to provide the company with at least $180 million, $100 million in the form of stock purchases in the company.

• State and local government bodies where Chrysler maintained manufacturing operations were required to provide $250 million in funds.

• New stock worth $50 million had to be issued and sold.

• Union employees of Chrysler had to sacifice $462.2 million (measured as concessions from the Big Three pattern contract), and non-union employees had to contribute $125 million in the form of pay cuts or freezes.

If Chrysler was able to meet these targets, it would exceed by far the $1.5 billion required by the Federal Government in order to borrow yet another $1.5 billion under the act with the government guarantee. Time was ticking away, however, and Chrysler's financial position was deteriorating further. There were those willing to give their lives to salvage Chrysler, as Riccardo almost did. But many others remained as skeptical about Chrysler's future with the law in hand as they were before the legislation was passed. From Iacocca's optimistic

File Photo from The Chrysler Corporation

The 1981 model year Dodge Aries and the Plymouth Reliant are the cars upon which the Chrysler corporation says its future rests. The new cars faced rough competition however from other domestic makers and foreign car manufacturers.

prediction that Chrysler's 1980 losses would be only
half-a-billion dollars, compared to the $1.1 billion it
then saw itself losing for all of 1979, to the reassurances
of Treasury Secretary Miller, the convert, that Chrysler's
future was now on a sound footing, something was wrong.
Too much, the skeptics felt, rested on too little in the
way of facts and on assurances from a group that had
only recently jumped on the bandwagon.

Chrysler's entire future rested on its success or
failure in the increasingly tough marketplace with a
single automobile — a new compact car to be offered
in the fall of 1980. Throughout the struggle in Washington
and the efforts to line up the contributions required by
the new law, Chrysler management maintained that the
K-Car was the key to solving its problems. But without
massive help, the company would not be able to stay
in business long enough to get the new car out of the
factory and onto the market. With the new law and the
concessions Chrysler was assured of being able to try
to successfully launch a car that, unlike so many others
of earlier years, was right for the times. It was visibly
small and considerably more competitive than its
predecessors with respect to fuel economy, and was able
to ride the coattails of the success that General Motors
was enjoying with its new compact, the X-Car. According
to Chrysler's market research, General Motors was unable
to meet the consumer demand for its X-Cars and Chrysler
hoped to pick up the slack. In addition, the cost of
manufacturing the K-Car would be considerably less
than Chrysler had spent on previous models because
most of the major components, including the engine,
would be built within the company. "Help us get the
car to market," Chrysler fund raisers told all involved.
"We know it will sell." It had to.

The K-Cars would constitute nearly 42 percent, just
under 500,000 units, of all of Chrysler's passenger car
production for the 1981 model year. With the cost per
vehicle down and small-car prices skyrocketing, the K-Car

was seen as yielding the highest profit margin for any vehicle Chrysler planned to sell in 1981, thereby significantly improving the prospective company's cash flow and potential for profits. The only exception in Chrysler's generally economy-oriented plan was a limited edition of 25,000 units — a new Imperial, a full-size luxury car.

To raise funds in short order, Iacocca and his finance chief, Gerald Greenwald, established 22 work teams. Each had a specific task: one handled suppliers, another dealers, another state and local governments, another Canada, and so on. Weekly, Friday was designated as review day, with the reports starting early in the morning and running past sundown. Points of progress, as well as trouble spots were closely examined and plans of action were mapped out for the following week. The routine continued weekly from January, 1980, until the last obstacle was knocked down.

The United Auto Workers, which already had cut its deal in Washington to scale down the sacrifices which Senate opponents were demanding, was the first to help Chrysler clear a major hurdle. In late January, Fraser and Stepp pushed through the second renegotiation of a Big Three pattern contract, extracting further concessions from Chrysler workers. That, again, was unprecedented in American labor history.

Within days of the union action, Chrysler had lined up the $125 million in concessions from its suppliers, even though many of them were also ailing because of the industry's protracted slide. Chrysler held the line on some prices, deferred billings and rolled back other prices. The company began to get tough with its suppliers, something many were not accustomed to, but the new law gave the company more muscle.

The governors of most of the key Chrysler states had supported the company's efforts in Washington from the start. The only exception was the governor of Alabama. Once the Federal legislation was adopted,

Michigan and the City of Detroit took the lead among government bodies in providing aid for Chrysler, raising close to $200 million through cash and investment tax credits. Indiana and Delaware also moved quickly to aid Chrysler. But opposition flared in other states, for a multitude of reasons, ranging from philosophical objections to public aid, to skepticism about the prudent value of helping Chrysler. The failure of some states to fall in line quickly was the first indication that trouble was brewing. The real sign, however, was Chrysler's trouble with its banks.

In addition to a handful of insurance companies with substantial loans to Chrysler, the company had lending agreements with about 400 banks worldwide. They were big-city banks and small-town banks, obscure banks and prestigious banks. Between the corporation and Chrysler Financial, $251.4 million was owed to the Prudential Insurance Company of America; Aetna Life was due $70.6 million and Blue Cross/Blue Shield of Michigan held notes for $50 million.

Basically, the bank lenders fell into one of two groups. The revolving lenders were the larger banks with largest amounts loaned to Chrysler for periods ranging from two to five years. The regular line banks were primarily the smaller institutions with small, short-term loans to Chrysler running from a day to no more than a year.

The smaller bank lenders had come to deal with Chrysler on terms negotiated individually, as had many of the larger institutions. When Chrysler sought to bundle them all into a single group to expedite the Chrysler aid campaign, the smaller banks bolted. Their actions were prompted by a series of developments dating back to early 1979.

In May, 1979, Chrysler reported a $53.8 million loss for the first three months of that year, with Riccardo telling reporters at his quarterly business conference that "the next quarter is going to be a rough quarter." In the following month, Chrysler invited representatives of all its lenders to a two-day gathering in Detroit and a tour of engineering and product planning operations at company headquarters in Highland Park. In the meetings, Chrysler's top brass brought out the company's books and gave the lenders two scenarios on the financial outlook for the year. Tier I was the optimistc outlook, while Tier II held the pessimistic view. The bankers were only interested in Tier II. What they saw shook them. The bad news, said Chrysler, was that the company expected substantial losses for all of 1979. The good news was that Chrysler felt the losses could be contained to about $391 million.

A month later, Riccardo went public with his bailout appeal and a projection that losses for the year were expected to be at least $1 billion. Immediately, the smaller banks wanted out, asserting that a bailout would only postpone what they saw as an inevitable bankruptcy. The larger banks froze some of their lines of credit. Gradually, more and more of the regular line banks notified Chrysler they wanted an immediate payment of their loans. Chrysler refused.

Meanwhile, in Washington, a committee of Chrysler lenders was organized to hammer out with Treasury officials the terms of a debt-restructuring component for the loan guarantee plan. Some of the most prestigious lenders in the financial community sat on the committee, such as Citibank, Manufacturers Hanover Trust and Prudential. But, to the dismay of the small, regular line lenders — whose total debt exposure was just under $70 million — none of their ranks was asked to serve on the committee, even in an advisory capacity. They were advised, in fact, that they would not have a role in designing the plan although they would be expected to abide by its terms once it was adopted as part of the loan guarantee legislation.

The snub infuriated the smaller banks, and their anger was heightened when the broad outlines of the plan agreed to in October, 1979, by the U.S. Treasury and the lenders committee was announced. The plan provided for interest concessions, forgiveness of some interest due and extended repayment terms. The regular line bankers charged that the big lenders gave away too much to an already lost cause. At the same time, the big lenders advised Chrysler that they would participate in the plan only if every lender to whom the company owed money took part. The big lenders were already fed up and in no mood to buy out the loans of the small bankers.

The small lenders' dissension turned into a loosely organized rebellion against a form of taxation without representation. It came from all over the country: the Bank of the Southwest National Association, Houston; the American National Bank and Trust Company, Rockford, Illinois; The Twin City Bank, North Little Rock, Arkansas; The Peoples Trust Bank, Fort Wayne, Indiana; The Crestwood Metro Bank, St. Louis. Their views also were shared by several foreign banks that had been excluded from the planning process. Most of the balking banks responded by refusing to sign the documents sent them, in which they were to agree to the terms of the refinancing plan.

Chrysler was unable to meet its much-publicized April 1 target date for presenting the government with evidence that it had lined up the necessary commitments needed to qualify for federally backed borrowing privileges.

By late spring, Chrysler was existing only on a day-to-day basis. It had used up every quick-fix source of money that it could find, including an infusion of some $150 million from the State of Michigan, $100 million borrowed from Peugeot, as Chrysler posted its 15 percent equity in the French auto maker as security, and deferrals on two different occasions of payments to suppliers. A standby emergency plan that Iacocca had said would be used only as a last resort was about to be called up if the holdout banks did not come through.

Under the plan, the White House would be called and told that the company would be in bankruptcy court in 36 hours unless the recalcitrant banks caved in.

In a sudden scramble toward the middle of June, 1980, an all-out effort was made to twist arms until they almost broke. Bank presidents began personal appeals to the heads of the holdout banks. Political persuasion was levied via personal calls from Secretary Miller to heads of each of the uncooperative banks. Similarly, state governors were brought into the fray. For example, Indiana's Governor Otis Bowen refused an Administration request that he intervene with the Peoples Trust Bank in Fort Wayne, despite having helped Chrysler in other ways, saying that the bank's decision to stay in or out of the deal was not his business. An effort was considered to get Leon Jaworski, the former Watergate prosecutor, to make a courtesy call on the officials at the Bank of the Southwest. One by one, the ranks of the holdouts began to shrink.

One of the last banks to reluctantly reverse its position and agree to go along with the debt plan was the American National Bank and Trust Company in Rockford, Illinois. Chrysler owed the institution $525,000. David W. Knapp, the bank's president, had been among the more outspoken of the dissenting bank executives, but said on the eve of his bank's decision to reverse itself that the switch was influenced mostly by two factors, "divisiveness in the community and the safety of our employees."

Knapp had won considerable praise for standing up in public against the big shots in New York, but was the target of much criticism as well. Workers at the Chrysler Belvidere Assembly Plant just up the road from Rockford picketed the bank and threatened a boycott. Bank officials received nasty phone calls, including two bomb threats. The situation was ironic, in a sense, because Chrysler workers at the Belvidere Plant were among the few United Auto Workers locals in the

Chrysler system to vote against the wage concessions mandated by the bailout plan. In addition, the Illinois legislature was among those balking at state aid to Chrysler. So what was wrong with the hometown bank standing its ground?

Though they had given in, Knapp and the other bankers would not concede. "The final chapter hasn't been written yet," Knapp would say.

June 24,1980, the day officials of the Loan Guarantee Board and Chrysler signed the official documents allowing the company to borrow $500 million with government backing, the first installment, was a day of much public jubilation in Washington, New York and Paris, where simultaneous signings of the relevant documents were staged. By nightfall, "the New Chrysler Corporation" was back in the money, but by no means a high roller.(*)

Even in the long, sterile, mortuary-like fifth-floor hallways of Chrysler headquarters, sighs of relief could be heard sweeping from the offices of the company's top executives. Elsewhere in the huge Chrylser complex, Margaret Neaton, who once worked as Charles Heinen's secretary, stopped in his office to tell him the good news. "We got it, Charlie," she announced. "I said 'okay,'" Heinen, Chrysler's director of research, materials and engineering, recalled, "and then just went back to work. I was happy to see it happen because if it hadn't — I could see 47 years of my life going down the drain."

But for Heinen, who had weathered many a storm with Chrysler since joining the auto maker in 1934 as a floor sweeper and retired only weeks later, it was a sad note on which to end his career. "All of this sounded real good logically, but emotionally it was a cruel blow."

---

* A table outlining the debt structure of the Chrysler Corporation before and after the Loan Guarantee Program is included in the Appendix.

Chapter 9

"*We used to be king of everything...*"

Philip Caldwell

By late 1980, Chrysler's successful bid to salvage itself as a much smaller, primarily North American automobile manufacturer had become part of a larger and more unsettling turn of events. The entire American automobile industry was sick, in serious financial and competitive trouble, and turning increasingly to the government and foreign sources for help. A key pillar upon which America rested was shaking at its foundation. With their spending programs on new products to meet government standards and world competition locked into place, the four major American-based automobile manufacturers faced combined losses for 1980 in excess of $4 billion, with Chrysler accounting for just over $1 billion. American-made vehicle sales were continuing to nosedive, as the industry slide spilled into its third consecutive model year under pressures from a sick economy and growing consumer demand for foreign cars, mostly those made in Japan (Toyota, Datsun and Honda). In a year that saw total industry sales fall by more than 20 percent, the foreign-car share of market sales would soar to nearly 30 percent.

The American automobile dealership network was falling apart, with some 1,500 dealers shutting their doors between January, 1979, and July, 1980, and hundreds of others surviving only by virtue of carrying foreign cars alongside the domestic makes. Automobile manufacturing and assembly plants — age-old institutions such as the Chrysler Hamtramck, Michigan, plant and more modern giants such as the Ford Motor Mahwah plant in New Jersey — were padlocked. Workers were laid off their jobs permanently by the thousands. The "troubled Chrysler" headlines that dominated newspapers and airwaves only weeks earlier had been changed to "troubled Detroit."

American Motors, which had begun to see the light of day in the late 1970's after repeated brushes with disaster, found itself bleeding at the seams by the mid-1980 with its American lenders unwilling to bankroll it any further through its hard times at hand. To avoid collapse, in the face of losses for its 1980 fiscal year of several million dollars, American Motors turned to its French-government owned partner, Renault, for a quick infusion of confidence and $200 million in cash. In return, Renault, which had already advanced American Motors $90 million in cash for an option to purchase 22 percent interest in the company, found itself entitled to a 46 percent interest in the small auto maker and taking active roles in key management areas at the Detroit-area based company.

Ford Motor, a worldwide automotive giant, found itself retrenching at home and borrowing funds at an unprecedented rate from every available source (including $1 billion in loans from its subsidiaries in Europe). To stay in the race in the marketplace, Ford turned to numerous automakers abroad — in Japan and Europe — to supply engines and other key automobile components it did not see itself able to produce.

General Motors, the industry giant that had boasted of rarely having to go outside its own bank account to finance its projects for the 1980's, faced the need to borrow billions to make cars that would meet the government demands and competitive bites head on.

Chrysler, looking toward restoration of just enough health to be considered a merger partner, was breathing only by the graces of its government respirator.

In sharp contrast, Volkswagen was launching construction of its second American assembly plant, this one in suburban Detroit.

With all new products coming into the market for the 1981 model year and each year thereafter until 1985, the American auto makers still faced the possibility that their products might not cut the mustard, given the higher criteria set by American car and truck buyers in an era governed by extreme sensitivity to vehicle prices, fuel supply and costs. To improve the chance of American-made cars in the marketplace, they demanded that the government limit competition by restricting the number of imports that could be sold in the nation for an indefinite period of time. To improve their cash flow positions, they were insisting that numerous government regulations on the industry, covering safety, air pollution and fuel economy, be quickly relaxed. They received support in their controversial demands for protection from the Japanese. And the government responded to the regulatory relief calls by dismantling numerous regulations of the 1960's and 1970's, particularly those related to clean air.

Both President Carter and Ronald Reagan, heading into the last phase of the 1980 presidential campaign as the two major nominees for president, proposed ambitious industry aid plans, including a version of the Chrysler tax credit advance plan that only a year earlier had been ridiculed as preposterous.

In the meantime, Japan was producing cars at record rates. These rates by year's end would bestow on that tiny nation the honor of producing more cars in a year than any other nation in the world. This was a serious blow to the pride of America, which had worn that crown since 1908. For the blow to have been delivered by Japan was especially embarrassing since it was the same nation which had been brought to its knees during World War II when hit with the devastating atomic bomb perfected by Chrysler; leadership loss meant rubbing salt in a wound. The opening shots of World War III, to be fought on the battlefields of commerce, had been heard, and again, America was not prepared.

"We used to be king of everything," Philip Caldwell, the new chairman of Ford Motor, would tell an audience of reporters as he recalled America's world posture at the end of World War II. "Now we've got people coming to America showing us how to do better the things that we taught them in the first place."

The industry that America has grown with over the past three generations is now a staggering giant. It has suffered from decisions by American business power brokers to run their companies on the short-term profit and gain motive, indifferent to developments beyond American shores until this policy proved a disaster. A new era is at hand, one in which American auto makers face a fate much like that of today's American railroad system — a small collage of strong, privately-held companies and several weaker, government-backed entities that may bleed the taxpayer indefinitely.

Free enterprise will kick and scream louder and the march to Washington will become more common in coming years. Companies, in search of massive cash infusions, will be subjected to public ridicule, as in the case of Chrysler, or forced into back-door concessions, such as tax abatements, free job training and land, as in the case of General Motors and healthier competitors. American free enterprise is threatened with impotence on the world level as the Federal Government rushes to the rescue of one industry after another. Abroad, it is viewed as only catching up with the new reality of world competition, one that does not draw its lines between government, labor and business so firmly that all choke as a result.

American automobile industry executives declared in the 1970's that the 1980's would be a crucial decade for the world automobile community and thus the world industrial community. It will be characterized by another shakeout in the automobile industry worldwide, with only six or eight manufacturers in existence by 1990. Only the strong will survive, they have predicted, with everyone competing in basically the same segment of the market — small, highly fuel-efficient vehicles. The cost of doing business will force the weak and marginal to close ranks via mergers and integrated ownership, or fall by the wayside. If that is the case, the once-impregnable American industry enters the ring as one of the weakest links in the chain. It is a frightening position to be in at such a crucial time in history.

The American visions of the decade of survival were predicated, as have so many of their views in the past, upon Detroit having a decisive say in the direction in which developments go and the pace at which they occur. In fact, much of what happens to America in the coming decade hinges upon developments beyond Detroit, beyond America.

The nation's mobility is in the hands of a foreign oil cartel. The partnerships of Chrysler and Rockefeller have given way to odd bedfellows: a powerful OPEC providing the muscle behind the American oil industry's efforts to deregulate prices on the 50 percent of domestic energy needs we still supply ourselves. And finally, the nation's standard of excellence in product quality rests on its ability to achieve the higher standards of excellence that most in the American industry agree are set by the Japanese, not General Motors.

Against such realities, there are stirrings about the nation of the need for coalitions of government, labor and business to forge a rebuilding of America in the 1980's, one that could put the country back in control of its destiny and restore its reputation for industrial integrity. The Chrysler bailout is symbolic of the mood and represents a crucial turning point in the finding of answers.

References

Much of the information for this book was gathered in personal interviews with dozens of people whose knowledge of various aspects of the industry and its relationship with the goverment and financial community proved of invaluable insight.

In addition, selected information published by the following organizations for public consumption was utilized in the research process:

The Detroit Free Press; American Road Builders and Transportation Association; Association of American Railroads; The Atlanta Constitution; Automotive Information Council; The Chrysler Corporation; Congress Watch; The Congressional Quarterly; Crain Communications Group; The Detroit Public Library; The Flint Journal; The Ford Dealer Alliance; The Ford Motor Company; The General Motors Corporation; The Independent Dealers Association Dedicated to Action.

Also, The Los Angeles Times; Merrill Lynch, Pierce Fenner & Smith, automotive group; The Motor Vehicle Manufacturers Association; The National Automobile Dealers Association, The New York Times; The Stockholders Committee for The Preservation of the Chrysler Corporation; The National Highway Traffic & Safety Administration; The United States Department of Treasury, The Wall Street Journal; Ward's Quarterly.

There are several books that also proved invaluable references for gaining an understanding of the varying perspectives on the history of this industry:

All Our Yesterdays; a History of Detroit. Frank and Arthur Woodford, Wayne State University Press, 1969.
American Odyssey. Robert Conot, Bantam, 1975.
American Heritage. (story by Stephen Sears), American Heritage, 1979.
Decade of Decision. Michael Harrington, Simon & Shuster, 1980.
The Dream Machine. Jerry Flint, Quadrangle, 1976.

The Lean Years. Richard Barnett, Simon & Shuster 1980.

Life of An American Worker. Walter Chrysler, Curtis, 1938.

Mankind at the Turning Point. Mesarovic and Pestel, Dutton, 1974.

My Years With General Motors. Alfred Sloan Jr., Doubleday, 1963.

On a Clear Day You Can See General Motors. Patrick Wright, Wright, 1979.

Also:

Reckless Homicide? Lee Strobel, and books, 1980.

Rememberances of Things Past. Stanley Brams, Trends, 1975.

Seventy Years of Chrysler. George Dammann, Crestline, 1974.

Unsafe at Any Speed. Ralph Nader, Grossman, 1965.

The War Against the Automobile. B. Bruce Briggs, Dutton, 1975.

What's Good for G.M. Edward Ayers, Aurora, 1970.

Appendix

Main Features of The Loan Guarantee Act

On May 10, 1980, the United States Department of the Treasury issued a "fact sheet" setting forth the basic points of the Chrysler Loan Guarantee Act and the assumptions the Chrysler Loan Guarantee Board made in giving conditional approval to Chrysler's financial operating plan and loan requests. The following are key excerpts from that report:

Financing Plan

The act requires at least $1.43 billion in non-Federally guaranteed financing in excess of commitments and concessions outstanding on October 17, 1979. The Board found that $227 million in commitments were outstanding on October 17, 1979, which have not been funded or replaced. It therefore required that an equal amount of additional non-Federally guaranteed financing be provided in the Financing Plan. The commitments that have not been extended and that have been made up by other financing, sales of assets or concessions consist of $159 million of revolving credit loans from U.S. banks and $68 million in lines of credit with Canadian banks.

Chrysler proposed a Financing Plan which included $2.4 billion in private, non-Federally guaranteed financing. The Board found reasonable assurance that $2.032 billion, would be received.

The Board agreed to modify the statutory targets for contributions from various parties as follows:

	Target	Plan of 4/29	Board Approval
New loans, credits or concessions from lenders, both domestic and foreign	650	680	642
Disposition of assets	300	723	628
State, local or other governments	250	399.5	357*
Suppliers and dealers	180	150	63
Sale of additional equity	50	0	0
Pension fund contribution deferral	0	456	342
Subtotal	1,430	2,409	2,032
Commitments not extended	227		
Total	1,657	2,409	2,032

(*) Omits portion of Canadian $10 million grant from Ontario for research because information on the timing of the grant is incomplete.

In approving $2.032 billion as meeting the statutory requirements, the Board made adjustments to the values placed by Chrysler on lender assistance, disposition of assets, assistance from suppliers and dealers, and deferrals of pension fund contributions.

The Board found that the financing contemplated by Chrysler's Financing Plan meets the needs of the company and that adequate assurances have been received with respect to the remaining portion of Chrysler's Financing Plan, the Board will require Chrysler to use its best efforts to obtain that financing on a timely basis and the Board will review its success in doing so in connection with the issuance of further loan guarantees.

The staff said the legislative history of the Act clearly indicates that adequate assurance that binding commitments will be forthcoming — not that they have already been made — is sufficient for the issuance of the guarantee commitment and that the determination of adequacy may be made by the Board in the exercise of reasonable business judgment.

Although the Financing Plan, as defined by the statute, is concerned with fiscal years 1980 through 1983, Chrysler's Plan provides for additional interest deferrals from certain of Chrysler's lenders valued at approximately $400 million which will be available after December 31, 1983, and the right to convert up to $750 million in interest deferrals into preferred stock, if Chrysler meets certain minimum goals.

The staff noted that the deferrals are the economic equivalent of new loans and the option to convert to preferred stock could provide Chrysler with up to $750 million in equity after December 31, 1983.

The staff's projections of Chrysler's earnings are lower than those upon which Chrysler's has projected its financial needs. Therefore, the expected use of Federal loan guarantees is higher and for a longer period of time than projected by Chrysler. However, even under the staff's conservative projections, a sufficient amount of Federal guarantees would remain available to provide a margin against unexpected developments.

A. Assistance from Lenders.

At present $1.869 billion in long and short term loans to Chrysler are outstanding. The Chrysler lenders include domestic, Canadian, Japanese and European banks and financial institutions. These lenders have agreed to extend maturities falling due before 1983, which provides financing of $154 million; to concede a portion of the interest payable valued by Chrysler at $181 million including interest on interest, and to defer payment of a portion of the remaining interest, valued at $345 million including interest on the deferrals. After making certain adjustment, the Board valued this assistance at $542 million.

With respect to the bulk of the loans outstanding, Chrysler will pay an aggregate interest rate of 15 percent consisting of cash interest of 5.5 percent, deferrals of seven percent and forgiveness of 2.5 percent. Lenders will receive interest-bearing notes for the deferred interest. In return for these concessions and deferrals, Chrysler's lenders will receive warrants to purchase 12 million shares of Chrysler's common stock at $13 a share, through 1990. The Board found that these warrants had only nominal values and did not have to be deducted from the value of the concessions.

Deferred principal repayments will be made over five or six years. — Amortization periods will commence on the later of March 31, 1984, or the date on which the federally guaranteed loans are paid in full. The deferred interest notes will be paid in 20 to 24 installments beginning on March 32, 1984; however, the maturities may be adjusted to provide for pro-rated payment with any Federally guaranteed loans outstanding after 1984.

Certain of the lenders have also agreed to grant Chrysler the option after 1983, if certain conditions are met, to continue to pay 5.5 percent interest in cash, and to defer the balance at a 15 percent annual rate of interest and to exchange up to $750 million in deferred interest notes for new preferred stock. The conditions for the exercise of this option are that Chrysler sell or have orders for 350,000 K cars in the 1981 model year (65 percent of projected capacity), that it not have a cumulative net operating loss of more than $500 million from July 1, 1981, through December 1, 1983, to the end of the deferral period and that it not become subject to a bankruptcy proceeding.

B. Sale of Assets.

Chrysler's Financing Plan provides for $320 million from the sale of 51 percent of the Chrysler Finance Corporation, $196 million from the sale of real estate, $100 million from a non-recourse loan from Peugeot (secured from Peugeot stock owned by Chrysler), and $56 million from sale of Chrysler Australia, $36.2 million from the sale of Chrysler Argentina, $14.3 million from sale of notes of Chrysler Brazil and $2 million from sale of Chrysler Boat.

Subject to certain conditions that staff expected to be met, the Board approved inclusion in the Financial Plan of the amounts projected from the sales of Chrysler Argentina, Chrysler Australia and the notes of Chrysler Brazil as well as the non-recourse loan from Peugeot. The sale of Chrysler Boat was not included at this time, pending receipt of additional information. The Board found adequate assurance that only $171.3 million would be realized from the sale of Chrysler's surplus real estate. The Board reached this figure after considering appraisals of the property but also the absence of firm offers and probable selling expenses. Moreover, the Board included $250 million from the proposed sale of 51 percent of the Chrysler Financial Corporation based upon a staff analysis and an opinion from Salomon Bros. that $250 million is the minimum a willing and able purchaser would be prepared to pay. Book value of Chrysler Financial Corporation is approximately $644 million. The Board approved asset sales in the amount of $628 million.

C. Assistance from State, local and other Governments.

The Financial Plan includes $187 million in secured loans from the states of Michigan ($150), Indiana ($32) and Delaware ($5), and $170 million (Canadian $200 million) in loan guarantees from the government of Canada. The Canadian funds would be available in 1982 and 1983 as progress payments for the renovation of van-wagon production facilities and would be paid back over five years starting in 1984. The Canadian government has also required warrants to purchase Chrysler's common stock. The Board approved inclusion of $357 million in government assistance in the Financing Plan.

Michigan has lent Chrysler the $150 million contemplated in the Plan at 5.5 percent interest and maturity on January 1, 1995. The loan is secured by a first mortgage on Chrysler's Trenton, Michigan engine plant and related equipment.

Pursuant to recent legislation, the Board for Depositories of the Indiana Public Deposits Insurance Fund has adopted a resolution expressing its intention to negotiate with Chrysler to invest $32 million — in Chrysler's five year mortgage notes. The notes would be secured by an addition to Chrysler's Kokomo, Indiana, plant and related machinery and equipment. They would bear interest at not less than the rate for comparable obligations and be dependent on the board waiving U.S. priority in the event of Chrysler's bankruptcy. The Board agreed to waive the U.S. priority for the investment by the Indiana Public Deposits Insurance Fund.

Delaware has enacted a statute authorizing a newly created Emergency Loan committee to lend $5 million to Chrysler. The 15-year loan, with interest at 15.5 percent for the first five years, would be secured by Chrysler's Delaware, Parts Depot and would be called if the Chrysler Assembly Plant in Newark, Delaware permanently ceased manufacturing operations.

D. Assistance from Dealers and Suppliers.

The Plan provides for $100 million in proceeds from the sale of 12 percent subordinated debentures to dealers, suppliers and others with an economic stake in Chrysler. These debentures may be purchased in 24 equal installments and are convertible into 8 percent preferred stock at the option of the holder. They have a maturity of 10 years and can be redeemed in equal installments beginning in the sixth year.

The Board agreed to include only $63 million from the proceeds of debenture sales. Through April, Chrysler had received signed subscriptions for $78.2 million that will become legally effective on resolicitation. Staff estimated that 80 percent of the subscriptions could be expected to be reaffirmed and recommended that only that amount of financing be counted as assured. It further recommended that only subscriptions that have become legally binding be counted at the time guarantees are issued.

The Plan includes an additional $50 million from the extension of payment terms with certain suppliers that will be negotiated over the next six to 12 months. However, the Board found that there was not adequate assurance of financing from the deferral of supplier payables and excluded that amount from the Plan.

E. Capital.

The Plan contemplates no sale of stock because a stock offering is considered impractical given the company's present condition and since the statute prohibits dividend payments while Federal loan guarantees are outstanding. As a result, the Board waived the requirement that $100 million be raised in the form of equity and capital. The staff noted that Chrysler's option to convert interest deferrals into preferred stock could provide up to $750 million in equity after 1983. Chrysler will commit itself to issue $100 million of new common or preferred stock as soon as practicable.

F. Deferred Pension Contributions.

The Plan proposes to use a provision of Chrysler's contract with the United Auto Workers that allows contributions to all employee funds to be deferred to the next year. This will provide a cash benefit of $308 million in 1980, rising to $456 million by 1983. The Board decided to include $342 million toward meeting the $1.43 billion requirement.

III. THE OPERATING PLAN.

The Board determined that Chrysler had submitted a "satisfactory" Operating Plan demonstrating the company's ability to continue operating as a going concern and to do so after 1983 without further Federal assistance. The Board determined that it had received adequate assurances that the operating plan is "realistic and feasible." Opinions were received from Chrysler and from its management consultant, Booz, Allen & Hamilton and its accounting firm, Touche Ross & Company, in addition to the analysis prepared by the staff.

A. Elements of the Plan.

The Plan, so revised on April 28, provides for a downsizing of the company and for accelerated introduction of new small, fuel efficient cars, with the K car on schedule for introduction in the fall of 1980. By model year 1984, Chrysler will produce only front wheel drive cars and trucks, powered predominantly by four cylinder engines.

The number of distinct vehicle lines will drop from five to three. There will be increased use of the same or similar parts on different vehicles, thus improving efficiency and facilitating service.

In the April Plan, Chrysler reduced the projected volume of rear wheel drive cars and trucks and adopted plans to consolidate van and bus production. The April Plan also simplified Chrysler's front wheel drive large car program by increasing the interchangeability of parts with the K car, thus decreasing expenditures on the program by about $1 billion. The revised Plan also provides for introduction of a small van and bus one year earlier than previously planned.

Fixed costs have been reduced by $122 million for 1980 by plant closings and layoffs, and variable margin improvements are expected, especially in connection with the introduction of the K car, but the size of these cost reductions has been scaled back from previous plans. Capital expenditures through 1985 have been reduced by approximately $1.5 billion compared to the plan submitted in February, and by about $2.5 billion from the December plan. For the 1979-85 period, they now total approximately $11.2 billion.

B. The Going Concern Test.

Although the staff's projections over the four year period are more conservative than Chrysler's by about $900 million, the staff advised that Chrysler is moving from a period of massive losses to one of modest earnings. Other considerations cited by the staff included:

• Chrysler is on the verge of introducing a new generation of small fuel-efficient cars that should position it in the segment of the highest demand in the auto market.

• By 1983, Chrysler will be a smaller, more efficient company with less overhead and a specialized product line.

• There is reason to assume that after 1983, Chrysler will be able to finance itself without further Federal financing assistance.

The staff also reported the availability of guaranteed or unguaranteed financing somewhat in excess of the levels required by its forecast providing a margin for unexpected developments.

The staff also presented various tests of the amount by which results could vary from its conservative forecast without exhausting the available financing. Based on these and other possible variations, the staff concluded that Chrysler would have a "reasonable financial margin against not fully achieving its plans and yet being in a position to achieve long-term viability."

D. Employee Concessions.

Based on analysis by an inter-agency task force hired by the Under Secretary of Labor, the Board detemined that the concessions made by unionized employees will save Chrysler $462.5 million in wages and benefits over the three-year life of the current labor contract signed on October 25, 1979. This includes a $203 million savings already in the original contract (that is, making it $203 million less favorable to Chrysler employees than settlements reached earlier by the United Auto Workers with Ford and General Motors). The additional $259.5 million in concessions were agreed to on January 5, 1980, after passage of the Act. These UAW concessions were followed by similar concessions made by the five other unions representing Chrysler employees.

The task force advised that the methodology and computions used by Chrysler in calculating the savings under these collective bargaining agreements are accurate and appropriate and meet the requirements of the Act.

Also based on review by the inter-agency task force, the Board found that Chrysler had adopted a plan that will result in an additional savings of $137.9 million by granting non-union employees salary and benefit improvements comparable to those of unionized employees.

E. Employee Stock Ownership.

The Board found that Chrysler has agreed to set up an employee stock ownership plan (ESOP) in return for the wage concessions accepted by Chrysler employees. The Corporation will contribute at least $162.5 million of common stock trust over four years starting July 4, 1980. An employee's stock and any accrued earnings may be cashed in upon death or other termination of employment with Chrysler. Chrysler has certified that the ESOP covers at least 90 percent of the employees who have accepted the wage concessions.

F. Prospect of Repayment.

The Board determined that there should be sufficient cash flow from 1980 through 1983 for Chrysler to continue operations as a going concern including the repayment of its debts as they become due after 1983 without resorting to additional loan guarantees or other Federal financing. After 1983, the corporation should also be able to meet all its capital requirements in the private market.

The Board further determined that the collateral to be pledged for the guaranteed loans, including inventory, accounts receivable, property, plants, equipment, investments, advances and equity in subsidiaries, will be reasonably sufficient to provide for repayment to the United States of the loans to be guaranteed.

G. Guarantee Fees.

The Board determined that the Act's requirement for guarantee fees was met by requiring a one percent fee on the average daily balance of guaranteed loans outstanding. The staff advised that the guarantee fee should more than cover government expenses of administering the Act, estimated at no more than $1.5 million a year. The Board also required warrants to purchase up to 18 million shares of Chrysler's common stock which can be exercised by the Board at $13 a share. The Board noted that appropriations would be required to exercise these warrants, thus ensuring a Congressional role in any decision to become a stockholder of Chrysler.

H. Relation of Guaranteed and Non-Guaranteed Assistance.

Fulfilling the statutory requirement that the amount of Federally guaranteed loans never exceed the acrued amount of non-federally guaranteed assistance, the Board determined in excess of $500 million in non-federally guaranteed assistance will have been obtained by Chrysler before the first $500 million in guarantees will be issued.

I. Waiver of Priority.

The Board agreed to waive the U.S. priority in bankruptcy with respect to $156 million in loans to Chrysler from the state of Michigan and the proposed $32 million loan from the Indiana Board of Public Depositories. The staff advised that the Michigan and Indiana loans were made to provide needed interim financing for Chrysler but would become immediately due if the waiver of priority were not granted. Chrysler certified that the loans could not have been obtained without the requested waiver of priority.

The Board also determined that the waiver did not affect its findings with respect to reasonable assurance of repayment of the guaranteed loans.

CHRYSLER CORPORATION DEBT

($ in Millions)

	June 30, 1979	June 30, 1980
United States and Canada		
Short Term Debt	$ 206	$ 106
Long Term Debt		
Public Issues	351	418
Banks	438	1,129
Insurance Companies	231	286
State Governments	—	150
U.S. Government Guaranteed	—	500
Miscellaneous	70	28
Subsidiaries Outside U.S. & Canada	180	150
Total Chrysler Corp. Debt	$ 1,476	$ 2,767

DEBT MATURITIES
BEFORE AND AFTER RESTRUCTURING -

($ in Millions)

	1980	1981	1982	1983	1984
Before Restructuring (June 30, 1979)	$ 492	$ 67	$ 88	$ 90	$ 95
After Restructuring* (June 30, 1980)	25	46	32	32	464
Cash Requirement Increase/(Decrease)	$(467)	$(21)	$(56)	$(58)	$ 369

Also, after the addition of $1,438 million of new debt financing and the elimination of $34 million of debt repayments due to the sale of Chrysler Australia.

Source: The Chrysler Corporation
September, 1980

Lending Institutions

On June 30, 1980, the Chrysler Corporation (referred to below as "CC") and the Chrysler Financial Corporation (referred to below as "CFC"), a wholly-owned subsidiary, listed the following institutions as lenders and stated the amounts due each creditor under one or more financial agreements.

CHRYSLER CORPORATION & CHRYSLER FINANCIAL CORPORATION
CREDIT FACILITIES ALPHABETIC SEQUENCE BY BANK

($ in Thousands)

NAME OF LENDER	LOCATION	Loans to CC	Loans to CFC	Total Loans
Albuquerque National Bank	Albuquerque, NM	–	650	650
Algemene Bank	Chicago, IL	20,720	18,250	38,970
Allied Bank International	New York, NY	–	2,000	2,000
Allied Irish Banks Limited	New York, NY	–	4,125	4,125
Allied Irish Investment Bank	Dublin, IR	–	3,000	3,000
American Express International	New York, NY	–	6,500	6,500
American Fletcher National Bank	Indianapolis, IN	2,376	3,900	6,276
American National Bank & Trust	Rockford, IL	–	650	650

NAME OF LENDER	LOCATION	Loans to CC	Loans to CFC	Total Loans
American National Bank & Trust	South Bend, IN	–	488	488
American Security Bank	Washington, DC	–	1,000	1,000
Ameritrust Company	Cleveland, OH	7,200	27,827	35,027
Ann Arbor Trust Company	Ann Arbor, MI	–	325	325
Atlantic Bank Of New York	New York, NY	–	500	500
Australia & New Zealand Bank Group	New York, NY	–	5,000	5,000
Banca Commerciale Italiana	Chicago, IL	11,000	5,000	16,000
Banco Atlantico	New York, NY	–	1,500	1,500
Banco De Bilbao	New York, NY	–	13,250	13,250
Banco Di Napoli	New York, NY	–	3,250	3,250
Banco Di Roma	Chicago, IL	10,000	6,500	16,500
Banco Di Vizcaya	New York, NY	5,000	–	5,000
Banco Do Brasil SA	New York, NY	–	2,000	2,000
Banco Nacional De Mexico	New York, NY	6,846	17,235	24,081
Bancohio National Bank	Columbus, OH	–	3,340	3,340
Bank Brussels Lambert Ltd.	London, UK	10,000	5,000	15,000
Bank Fuer Gemeinwirtschaft	New York, NY	10,000	9,650	19,650
Bank Of America NT & SA	New York, NY	21,600	161,001	182,601
Bank Of British Columbia	San Francisco, CA	400	6,680	7,080
Bank Of Commerce	Hamtramck, MI	1,000	325	1,325
Bank Of Ireland	Dublin, IR	–	3,000	3,000
Bank Of Lansing	Lansing, MI	–	650	650
Bank Of Montreal	New York, NY	65,000	52,650	117,650

NAME OF LENDER	LOCATION	Loans to CC	Loans to CFC	Total Loans
Bank Of Oklahoma	Tulsa, OK	1,080	975	2,055
Bank Of St. Louis	St. Louis, MO	360	325	685
Bank Of The Commonwealth	Detroit, MI	1,440	4,900	6,340
Bank Of The Southwest	Houston, TX	1,000	2,600	3,600
Bank Of The West	San Jose, CA	–	1,625	1,625
Bank Of Virginia	Richmond, VA	–	1,000	1,000
Bank Sanaye Iran	New York, NY	3,600	–	3,600
Bankers Trust Company	New York, NY	21,600	78,384	99,984
Bankers Trust Company of W. NY	Jamestown, NY	–	650	650
Bankers Trust Company	Albany, NY	–	1,300	1,300
Bankers Trust Company	Des Moines, IA	–	975	975
Banque De L Indochine Et Suez	Chicago, IL	6,800	–	6,800
Banque De L Union Europeenne	New York, NY	5,000	10,000	15,000
Banque Francaise Du Commerce	New York, NY	5,000	16,500	21,500
Banque Nationale De Paris	Chicago, IL	22,320	18,400	40,720
Banque Romande	Geneva, SW	5,000	–	5,000
Banque Rothschild	Paris, FR	–	5,000	5,000
Barclays Bank International	New York, NY	29,929	8,250	38,179
Bayerische Hypotheken Bank	New York, NY	–	10,000	10,000
Bayerische Landesbank Intl.	Luxembourg, LX	–	10,000	10,000
Boatmen's Union National Bank	Springfield, MO	–	250	250
California First Bank	San Francisco, CA	–	3,250	3,250
Canadian Imperial Bank Of Commerce	New York, NY	33,100	52,650	85,750

NAME OF LENDER	LOCATION	Loans to CC	Loans to CFC	Total Loans
Capital City FNB	Tallahassee, FL	—	195	195
Central Bank	Oakland, CA	—	2,000	2,000
Central National Bank Of Cleveland	Cleveland, OH	—	3,250	3,250
Central National Bank	Chicago, IL	—	2,450	2,450
Central Trust Company	Rochester, NY	—	1,475	1,475
Century Bank	Los Angeles, CA	—	300	300
Chemical Bank	New York, NY	18,000	96,083	114,083
Citibank	New York, NY	19,946	38,160	58,106
Citizens Fidelity Bank & Trust	Louisville, KY	—	1,475	1,475
City National Bank	Detroit, MI	1,800	1,800	3,600
City National Bank	Baton Rouge, LA	—	650	650
Commerce Bank of Kansas City	Kansas City, MO	720	1,300	2,020
Commerce Union Bank	Nashville, TN	—	1,625	1,625
Commercial National Bank	Little Rock, AR	—	650	650
Commercial National Bank	Shreveport, LA	—	650	650
Commercial Security Bank	Salt Lake, UT	—	650	650
Commerzbank AG	Chicago, IL	5,000	3,250	8,250
Continental Illinois NB & TR	Chicago, IL	16,560	81,966	98,526
Continental National Bank	Fort Worth, TX	—	1,300	1,300
Corpus Christi Bank & Trust	Corpus Christi, TX	—	650	650
Credit Commercial De France	New York, NY	—	5,000	5,000
Credit Industriel	New York, NY	—	5,000	5,000
Credit Lyonnais	Chicago, IL	21,000	13,000	34,000

NAME OF LENDER	LOCATION	Loans to CC	Loans to CFC	Total Loans
Credit Suisse	New York, NY	5,000	10,000	15,000
Credito Italiano	New York, NY	–	7,500	7,500
Crestwood Metro Bank	St. Louis, MO	250	–	250
Crocker National Bank	San Francisco, CA	7,200	58,832	66,032
Dai-Ichi Kangyo Bank LTD	New York, NY	13,352	3,250	16,602
Dakota Northwestern Bank	Bismarck, ND	–	488	488
Davenport Bank & Trust Comp	Davenport, IA	–	975	975
Delaware Trust Company	Wilmington, DE	360	–	360
Detroit Bank & Trust Company	Detroit, MI	4,680	26,541	31,221
Deutsche Genossenschafts Bank	New York, NY	8,600	14,750	23,350
Dresdner Bank AG	Chicago, IL	27,000	5,000	32,000
Easton National Bank & Trust	Easton, PA	–	325	325
El Paso National Bank	El Paso, TX	–	975	975
Empire National Bank	New York, NY	–	500	500
European American Banking Corp.	New York, NY	80,000	32,500	112,500
European American Bank & Trust	New York, NY	3,600	14,225	17,825
Farmers & Merchants Bank	Cape Girardeau, MO	–	163	163
Fidelity Union Trust Company	Newark, NJ	2,520	5,200	7,720
First Eastern Bank	Wilkes-Barre, PA	720	1,300	2,020
First Independence	Detroit, MI	–	465	465
First Pennsylvania Bank	Philadelphia, PA	9,432	14,805	24,237
First Alabama Bank	Montgomery, AL	1,000	650	1,650
First Bank	New Haven, CT	360	1,405	1,765

NAME OF LENDER	LOCATION	Loans to CC	Loans to CFC	Total Loans
First Bank	Minneapolis, MN	2,160	5,620	7,780
First Bank	Milwaukee, WI	720	1,300	2,020
First City Bank	Dallas, TX	—	1,950	1,950
First City National Bank	Houston, TX	3,600	6,500	10,100
First City National Bank	El Paso, TX	—	650	650
First National Bank	Totowa, NJ	—	1,000	1,000
First National Bank	Cincinnati, OH	720	975	1,695
First National Bank	Darlington, SC	—	650	650
First National Bank	Chicago, IL	16,560	62,286	78,846
First National Bank	Elkhart, IN	—	845	845
First National Bank	Louisville, KY	720	1,950	2,670
First National Bank & Trust	Marquette, MI	—	163	163
First National Bank	St. Paul, MN	2,376	4,225	6,601
First National Bank	Duluth, MN	—	650	650
First National Bank & Trust	Lincoln, NB	360	650	1,010
First National Bank	St. Louis, MO	2,880	5,200	8,080
First National Bank	Clayton, MO	—	325	325
First National Bank	Wichita, KS	—	650	650
First National Bank & Trust	Oklahoma City, OK	1,500	1,950	3,450
First National Bank	Dallas, TX	3,960	6,500	10,460
First National Bank	Lubbock, TX	—	975	975
First National Bank	Amarillo, TX	—	1,500	1,500
First National Bank	Great Falls, MT	360	—	360

NAME OF LENDER	LOCATION	Loans to CC	Loans to CFC	Total Loans
First National Bank	Reno, NV	—	650	650
First National Bank	Portland, OR	2,000	1,950	3,950
First National Bank	Casper, WY	—	650	650
First National State Bank	Newark, NJ	2,000	3,250	5,250
First Security Bank	Boise, ID	—	650	650
First Security Bank	Salt Lake, UT	1,000	2,625	3,625
First Tennessee Bank	Memphis, TN	2,520	1,800	4,320
First Wisconsin National Bank	Milwaukee, WI	2,000	4,900	6,900
First Wisconsin National Bank	Madison, WI	500	650	1,150
Fort Wayne National Bank	Ft. Wayne, IN	—	350	350
Garden State National Bank	Hackensack, NJ	—	1,000	1,000
Genossenschaftliche Zentralbk	Vienna, AU	—	5,000	5,000
Girard Bank	Philadelphia, PA	7,200	31,627	38,827
Golden State Sanwa Bank	San Francisco, CA	—	5,000	5,000
Gulf National Bank	Gulfport, MS	—	263	263
Harris Trust & Savings Bank	Chicago, IL	2,376	11,221	13,597
Hartford National Bank & Trust	Hartford, CT	720	1,650	2,370
Heritage/Pullman Bank & Trust	Chicago, IL	—	1,000	1,000
Illinois National Bank & Trust	Rockford, IL	—	650	650
Industrial BK of Japan TR Comp	New York, NY	—	3,000	3,000
Industrial National Bank	Providence, RI	1,000	3,250	4,250
Iowa-Des Moines National Bank	Des Moines, IA	720	1,300	2,020
Irving Trust Company	New York, NY	7,200	47,744	54,944

NAME OF LENDER	LOCATION	Loans to CC	Loans to CFC	Total Loans
J Henry Schroder Bank & Trust	New York, NY	—	4,300	4,300
Japan California Bank	Los Angeles, CA	1,080	500	1,580
Key Bank	Albany, NY	720	1,800	2,520
Key Bank of Central NY	Syracuse, NY	720	1,150	1,870
Kleinwort Benson Limited	London, UK	—	7,500	7,500
Kredietbank NV	New York, NY	—	8,000	8,000
Landesbank Rheinland-Pfalz GZ	Mainz, GE	—	25,000	25,000
Landmark First National Bank	Ft. Lauderdale, FL	—	650	650
Landmark Union Trust Bank	St. Petersburgh, FL	—	1,000	1,000
Lasalle National Bank	Chicago, IL	—	2,950	2,950
Liberty National Bank & Trust	Louisville, KY	—	1,475	1,475
Lincoln First Bank	Rochester, NY	—	4,175	4,175
Lincoln National Bank & Trust	Ft. Wayne, IN	—	650	650
London & Continental Bankers	London, UK	5,000	5,000	10,000
Manufacturers & Traders Trust	Buffalo, NY	—	1,650	1,650
Manufacturers Hanover Trust Co	New York, NY	33,800	178,095	211,895
Manufacturers Hanover Trust Co	Latham, NY	—	650	650
Manufacturers National Bank	Detroit, MI	3,960	26,217	30,177
Marine Midland Bank	New York, NY	12,240	28,771	41,011
Marine National Exchange Bank	Milwaukee, WI	720	1,650	2,370
Maryland National Bank	Baltimore, MD	1,440	—	1,440
Mellon Bank	Pittsburgh, PA	7,200	11,417	18,617
Mercantile National Bank	Dallas, TX	—	975	975
Mercantile Trust Company	St. Louis, MO	2,376	6,200	8,576

NAME OF LENDER	LOCATION	Loans to CC	Loans to CFC	Total Loans
Merchandise National Bank	Chicago, IL	—	325	325
Merchants National Bank & Trust	Indianapolis, IN	1,440	4,250	5,690
Michigan National Bank	Detroit, MI	3,520	2,275	5,795
Michigan National Bank	Lansing, MI	—	8,000	8,000
Midland National Bank	Minneapolis, MN	—	910	910
Midlantic National Bank	Newark, NJ	1,440	650	2,090
Morgan Guaranty Trust Co	New York, NY	17,424	96,083	113,507
National Bank of Canada	New York, NY	15,700	23,300	39,000
National Bank of Commerce	San Antonio, TX	360	1,800	2,160
National Bank of Detroit	Detroit, MI	8,640	71,482	80,122
National Bank of North America	New York, NY	4,752	8,800	13,552
National City Bank	Cleveland, OH	2,160	5,200	7,360
Nederlandsche Middestandsbank	New York, NY	—	5,000	5,000
Nevada National Bank	Reno, NV	—	650	650
New England Merchants	Boston, MA	720	3,600	4,320
New Jersey Bank	Paterson, NJ	2,000	1,950	3,950
North Carolina National Bank	Charlotte, NC	1,440	3,250	4,690
Northwest NB of Chicago	Chicago, IL	—	650	650
Northwestern National Bank	Minneapolis, MN	2,000	5,200	7,200
Northwestern National Bank	St. Paul, MN	—	1,405	1,405
Old National Bank	Evansville, IN	360	650	1,010
Orion Bank Limited	London, UK	—	5,000	5,000
Pacesetter Bank & Trust Company	Owosso, MI	—	445	445

NAME OF LENDER	LOCATION	Loans to CC	Loans to CFC	Total Loans
Pacific National Bank of Washington	Seattle, WA	–	1,300	1,300
Peoples Bank and Trust Company	Rocky Mt., NC	–	325	325
Peoples Trust Bank	Ft. Wayne, IN	1,000	650	1,650
Pioneer Bank & Trust Company	Chicago, IL	–	1,300	1,300
Pittsburgh National Bank	Pittsburgh, PA	3,600	6,500	10,100
Pontiac State Bank	Pontiac, MI	–	325	325
Provident National Bank	Philadelphia, PA	–	5,250	5,250
Ranier National Bank	Seattle, WA	1,440	1,300	2,740
Republic National Bank of NY	New York, NY	1,800	–	1,800
Republic National Bank	Dallas, TX	3,168	5,200	8,368
Rhode Island Hospital Trust	Providence, RI	500	2,300	2,800
Riggs National Bank of Washington	Washington DC	2,160	8,575	10,735
Seattle-First National Bank	Seattle, WA	4,160	6,500	10,660
Second National Bank	Saginaw, MI	360	1,040	1,400
Security Bank & Trust Company	Southgate, MI	–	650	650
Security First National Bank	Sheboygan, WI	–	1,300	1,300
Security National Bank of KC	Kansas City, KS	720	1,000	1,720
Security Pacific National Bank	Los Angeles, CA	10,800	58,940	69,740
Security Trust Company of Rochester	Rochester, NY	1080	–	1,080
Shawmut Bank of Boston	Boston, MA	2160	3,600	5,760
Slavenburg Overseas Banking Co.	Rotterdam, NE	–	5,000	5,000
Southeast First National Bank	Miami, FL	720	1,650	2,370
Springfield Marine Bank	Springfield, IL	–	1,300	1,300

NAME OF LENDER	LOCATION	Loans to CC	Loans to CFC	Total Loans
St. Joseph Bank And Trust Company	South Bend, IN	—	325	325
St. Louis County Bank	Clayton, MO	—	325	325
Standard Chartered Bank Ltd.	Chicago, IL	—	8,250	8,250
State Bank of Albany	Albany, NY	—	1,625	1,625
State National Bank	El Paso, TX	500	1,300	1,800
State Street Bank and Trust Co.	Boston, MA	—	3,250	3,250
Sun First National Bank	Orlando, FL	360	—	360
Swiss Bank Corporation	Chicago, IL	20,000	29,750	49,750
Texas Commerce Bank	Houston, TX	2,880	14,750	17,630
The First National Bank	Boston, MA	5,040	30,232	35,272
The First National Bank	Allentown, PA	—	1,300	1,300
The Northern Trust Company	Chicago, IL	3,888	16,021	19,909
The Bank of California	San Francisco, CA	1,440	3,250	4,690
The Bank of New Jersey	Camden, NJ	—	2,000	2,000
The Bank of New York	New York, NY	3,600	21,400	25,000
The Bank of Nova Scotia	New York, NY	23,000	57,850	80,850
The Bank of Tokyo Trust Company	New York, NY	17,363	3,250	20,613
The Boatmen's National Bank	St. Louis, MO	1,080	250	1,330
The Calcasieu-Marine Bank	Lake Charles, LA	—	650	650
The Capital National Bank	Austin, TX	—	650	650
The Chase Manhattan Bank	New York, NY	17,280	39,833	57,113
The Chuo Trust and Banking Co.	Tokyo, JA	1,760	—	1,760
The Citizens and Southern Bank	Atlanta, GA	1,000	4,550	5,550
The Connecticut Bank and Trust	Hartford, CT	—	1,000	1,000

NAME OF LENDER	LOCATION	Loans to CC	Loans to CFC	Total Loans
The Equitable Trust Company	Baltimore' MD	–	1,500	1,500
The Fidelity Bank	Philadelphia, PA	3,600	7,025	10,625
The Fifth Third Bank	Cincinnati, OH	720	2,600	3,320
The First Huntington Bank	Huntington, WV	–	250	250
The FNB of Denver	Denver, CO	720	–	720
The Fort Worth National Bank	Fort Worth, TX	720	–	720
The Goodyear Bank	Akron, OH	–	650	650
The Harter Bank & Trust Co.	Canton, OH	–	1,250	1,250
The Hibernia Bank	San Francisco, CA	–	488	488
The Hibernia National Bank	New Orleans, LA	500	975	1,475
The HongKong & Shanghai Bank	San Francisco, CA	–	3,250	3,250
The Huntington National Bank	Columbus, OH	–	1,800	1,800
The Idaho First National Bank	Boise, ID	–	1,550	1,550
The Indiana National Bank	Indianapolis, IN	1,800	3,900	5,700
The Industrial Bank Of Japan	New York, NY	18,045	–	18,045
The Lubbock National Bank	Lubbock, TX	–	400	400
The Mahoning National Bank	Youngstown, OH	–	650	650
The Merchants National Bank	Syracuse, NY	720	738	1,458
The Merchants National Bank	Muncie, IN	–	163	163
The Mitsubishi Bank LTD	Chicago, IL	38,495	–	38,495
The Mitsubishi Trust and Banking	New York, NY	39,587	–	39,587
The Mitsui Bank LTD	New York, NY	14,400	4,250	18,650
The National Bank And Trust Co	South Bend, IN	–	650	650

NAME OF LENDER	LOCATION	Loans to CC	Loans to CFC	Total Loans
The National Westminster Bank	Chicago,IL	16,000	23,400	39,400
The Nippon Trust and Banking Co.	Tokyo,JA	1,760	—	1,760
The Ohio Citizens Trust Co.	Toledo, OH	720	650	1,370
The Omaha National Bank	Omaha, NB	1,000	1,300	2,300
The Park National Bank	Knoxville, TN	—	1,300	1,300
The Philadelphia National Bank	Philadelphia,PA	2,880	9,800	12,680
The Royal Bank of Canada	New York, NY	44,600	54,400	99,000
The Sumitomo Trust and Banking Co.	Tokyo, JA	4,400	—	4,400
The Taiyo Kobe Bank LTD	New York, NY	26,921	—	26,921
The Tokai Bank LTD	New York, NY	19,227	5,000	24,227
The Toledo Trust Company	Toledo, OH	—	975	975
The Toronto Dominion Bank	New York, NY	34,900	52,650	87,550
The Toyo Trust and Banking Co.	Tokyo, JA	2,640	—	2,640
The Twin City Bank	North Little Rock, AR	—	780	780
The Yasuda Trust and Banking Co.	Tokyo, JA	2,640	—	2,640
The York Bank and Trust Company	York PA	—	2,000	2,000
The Third National Bank of Hampdon	Springfield, MA	500	975	1,475
The Third National Bank & Trust Co.	Dayton, OH	860	650	1,510
The Third National Bank in Nashville	Nashville, TN	—	1,300	1,300
Trinkaus & Burkhardt	Luxembourg, LX	—	10,000	10,000
UBAF Arab American Bank	New York, NY	—	5,000	5,000
Union Bank	Los Angeles, CA	3,000	5,000	5,000
Union Bank & Trust	Kokomo, IN	432	4,550	7,550

NAME OF LENDER	LOCATION	Loans to CC	Loans to CFC	Total Loans
Union Bank & Trust Company	Grand Rapids, MI	—	650	650
Union Bank of Bavaria	New York, NY	—	24,750	24,750
Union Commerce Bank	Cleveland, OH	1,720	3,900	5,620
Union National Bank	Lowell, MA	—	488	488
Union National Bank	Little Rock, AR	—	650	650
Union Trust Company of Maryland	Baltimore, MD	1,440	—	1,440
United American Bank	Knoxville, TN	—	650	650
United Bank Alaska	Anchorage, AK	—	195	195
United California Bank	Los Angeles, CA	7,920	19,671	27,591
United Penn Bank	Wilkes-Barre, PA	—	1,300	1,300
United States National Bank	Portland, OR	—	5,200	5,200
United States Trust Company	New York, NY	1,800	9,900	11,700
United Virginia Bank	Richmond, VA	—	1,625	1,625
Valley National Bank	Phoenix, AZ	720	3,250	3,970
Wachovia Bank and Trust Co.	Winston-Salem, NC	2,160	—	2,160
Walker Bank & Trust Co.	Salt Lake City, UT	720	1,300	2,020
Wells Fargo Bank	San Francisco, CA	1,000	3,250	4,250
Westfalenbank AG*	Bochum, GE	—	5,000	5,000
Whitney National Bank	New Orleans, LA	—	1,300	1,300
Winters National Bank & Trust	Dayton, OH	—	1,300	1,300
Zions First National Bank	Salt Lake City, UT	—	488	488

LOANS FROM MAJOR INSURANCE LENDERS

($ in Millions)

NAME OF LENDER	Loans to CC	Loans to CFC	Total Loans
Prudential Insurance Company of America	175	76.4	251.4
Aetna Life & Casualty	56.5	14.1	70.6
Blue Cross/Blue Shield of Michigan	50.0	NA	50.0

How They Voted

On December 18, 1979, the United States House of Representatives voted 271 to 136 in favor of adopting the Chrysler Loan Guarantee Act of 1979, and on the following day, the United States Senate voted 53 to 44 in favor of the measure — a $3.5 billion debt restructuring package for the Chrysler Corporation, including a guarantee from the Government that it would repay up to $1.5 billion in new loans made to Chrysler under the terms of the law. The Chrysler Loan Guarantee Act, as it is called, was passed as House Resolution 5860 and Public Law 96-185.

The following is a listing of how each member of the House and Senate voted on the final legislation by state and in the case of Representatives by Congressional District. The letter Y represents a yes vote; N, a no vote; C, present to avoid a possible conflict of interest; ? did not vote or make a position known; —, paired for. Republicans are identified in face print.

House Vote

ALABAMA		12 McCloskey	N	COLORADO	
1 Edwards	N	13 Mineta	Y	I Schroeder	N
2 Dickinson	N	14 Shumway	N	2 Wirth	N
3 Nichols	N	15 Coelho	Y	3 Kogovsek	Y
4 Bevill	N	16 Panetta	N	4 Johnson	Y
5 Flippo	Y	17 Pashayan	Y	5 Kramer	Y
6 Buchanan	Y	18 Thomas	N	CONNECTICUT	
7 Shelby	N	19 Lagomarsino	N	1 Cotter	Y
ALASKA		20 Goldwater	N	2 Dodd	Y
1 Young	Y	21 Corman	Y	3 Guamo	?
ARIZONA		22 Moorhead	Y	4 McKinney	Y
1 Rhodes	N	23 Beilenson	N	5 Ratchford	Y
2 Udall	Y	24 Waxman	Y	6 Moffett	Y
3 Stump	N	25 Roybal	Y	DELAWARE	
4 Rudd	N	26 Rousselot	N	1 Evans	Y
ARKANSAS		27 Dornan	N	FLORIDA	
1 Alexander	?	28 Dixon	Y	1 Hutto	Y
2 Bethune	N	29 Hawkins	Y	2 Fuqua	Y
3 Hammerschmidt	N	30 Danielson	Y	3 Bennett	N
4 Anthony	N	31 Wilson, C.H.	Y	4 Chappell	Y
CALIFORNIA		32 Anderson	Y	5 Kelly	N
1 Johnson	Y	33 Grisham	N	6 Young	N
2 Clausen	Y	34 Lungren	N	7 Gibbons	N
3 Matsui	Y	35 Lloyd	Y	8 Ireland	Y
4 Fazio	Y	36 Brown	Y	9 Nelson	Y
5 Burton, J.	Y	37 Lewis	N	10 Bafalis	N
6 Burton, P.	—	38 Patterson	Y	11 Mica	N
7 Miller	Y	39 Dannemeyer	N	12 Stack	Y
8 Dellums	Y	40 Badham	N	13 Lehman	?
9 Stark	X	41 Wilson, B.	?	14 Pepper	Y
10 Edwards	?	42 Van Deerlin	?	15 Fascell	Y
11 Royer	Y	43 Burgener	N		

GEORGIA	
1 Ginn	—
2 Mathis	Y
3 Brinkley	Y
4 Levitas	N
5 Fowler	Y
6 Gingrich	N
7 McDonald	N
8 Evans	Y
9 Jenkins	Y
10 Barnard	N
HAWAII	
1 Heftel	Y
2 Akaka	—
IDAHO	
1 Symms	X
2 Hansen	Y
ILLINOIS	
1 Stewart	Y
2 Murphy	?
3 Russo	Y
4 Derwinski	Y
5 Fary	Y
6 Hyde	Y
7 Collins	Y
8 Rostenkowski	Y
9 Yates	?
10 Mikva	—
11 Annunzio	Y
12 Crane,P.	X
13 McClory	Y
14 Erlenborn	N
15 Corcoran	N
16 Anderson	N
17 O'Brien	Y
18 Michel	N
19 Railsback	Y
20 Findley	N
21 Madigan	Y
22 Crane, D.	N
23 Price	Y
24 Simon	—
INDIANA	
1 Benjamin	Y
2 Fithian	Y
3 Brademas	Y
4 Quayle	Y
5 Hillis	Y
6 Evans	Y
7 Myers	Y
8 Deckard	Y

9 Hamilton	Y
10 Sharp	Y
11 Jacobs	Y
IOWA	
1 Leach	Y
2 Tauke	N
3 Grassley	Y
4 Smith	Y
5 Harkin	N
6 Bedell	Y
KANSAS	
1 Sibelius	?
2 Jeffries	N
3 Winn	Y
4 Glickman	N
5 Whittaker	N
KENTUCKY	
1 Hubbard	Y
2 Natcher	Y
3 Mazzoli	Y
4 Snyder	N
5 Carter	Y
6 Hopkins	N
7 Perkins	Y
LOUISIANA	
1 Livingston	N
2 Boggs	Y
3 Treen	?
4 Leach	Y
5 Huckaby	Y
6 Moore	N
7 Breaux	Y
8 Long	Y
MAINE	
1 Emery	N
2 Snowe	N
MARYLAND	
1 Bauman	N
2 Long	N
3 Milulski	Y
4 Holt	X
5 Spellman	Y
6 Byron	Y
7 Mitchell	Y
8 Barnes	N
MASSACHUSETTS	
1 Conte	Y
2 Boland	Y
3 Early	N
4 Drinan	Y
5 Sannon	Y

6 Mavroules	Y
7 Markey	Y
8 O'Neill	
9 Moakley	Y
10 Heckler	Y
11 Donnelly	Y
12 Studds	Y
MICHIGAN	
1 Conyers	Y
2 Pursell	Y
3 Wolpe	Y
4 Stackman	N
5 Sawyer	Y
6 Carr	Y
7 Kildee	Y
8 Traxler	Y
9 Vander Jaag	Y
10 Albosta	Y
11 Davis	Y
12 Bonior	Y
13 Diggs	Y
14 Nedzi	Y
15 Ford	Y
16 Dingell	Y
17 Brodhead	Y
18 Blanchard	Y
19 Broomfield	Y
MINNESOTA	
1 Erdahl	N
2 Hagedorn	N
3 Frenzel	N
4 Vento	Y
5 Sabo	Y
6 Nolan	Y
7 Strangeland	Y
8 Oberstar	Y
MISSISSIPPI	
1 Whitten	Y
2 Bowen	N
3 Montgomery	N
4 Hinson	Y
5 Lott	N
MISSOURI	
1 Clay	Y
2 Young	Y
3 Gephardt	Y
4 Skelton	Y
5 Bolling	Y
6 Coleman	N
7 Taylor	N
8 Ichard	N

9 Volkmer	Y	17 Murphy	Y	13 Pease	Y
10 Burlison	Y	18 **Green**	N	14 Seiberling	Y
MONTANA		19 Rangel	Y	15 **Wylie**	Y
1 Williams	Y	20 Weiss	Y	16 **Regula**	N
2 **Marlenee**	Y	21 Garcia	Y	17 **Ashbrook**	N
NEBRASKA		22 Bingham	Y	18 Applegate	Y
1 **Bereuter**	Y	23 Peyser	Y	19 **Williams**	Y
2 Cavanaugh	N	24 Ottinger	Y	20 Oakar	Y
3 **Smith**	N	25 **Fish**	Y	21 Stokes	Y
NEVADA		26 **Gilman**	Y	22 Vanik	Y
1 Santini	N	27 McHugh	Y	23 Mottl	C
NEW HAMPSHIRE		28 Stratton	Y	**OKLAHOMA**	
1 D'Amours	N	29 **Solomon**	N	1 Jones	N
2 **Cleveland**	N	30 **McEwen**	N	2 Synar	N
NEW JERSEY		31 **Mitchell**	Y	3 Watkins	N
1 Florio	Y	32 Hanley	Y	4 Steed	Y
2 Hughes	Y	33 **Lee**	Y	5 **Edwards**	N
3 Howard	Y	34 **Horton**	Y	6 English	N
4 Thompson	Y	35 **Conable**	N	**OREGON**	
5 Fenwick	Y	36 LaFalce	Y	1 AuCoin	N
6 **Forsythe**	Y	37 Nowak	Y	2 Ullman	Y
7 Maguire	N	38 **Kemp**	N	3 Duncan	Y
8 Roe	Y	39 Lundine	Y	4 Weaver	N
9 **Hollenbeck**	Y	**NORTH CAROLINA**		**PENNSYLVANIA**	
10 Rodino	Y	1 Jones	Y	1 Myers	Y
11 Minish	Y	2 Fountain	N	2 Gray	Y
12 **Rinaldo**	Y	3 Whitley	Y	3 Lederer	Y
13 **Courter**	N	4 Andrews	Y	4 **Dougherty**	Y
14 Guarini	Y	5 Neal	N	5 **Schulze**	N
15 Patten	Y	6 Preyer	Y	6 Yatron	Y
NEW MEXICO		7 Rose	N	7 Edgar	Y
1 **Lujan**	N	8 Hefner	N	8 Kostmayer	Y
2 Runnels	N	9 **Martin**	N	9 **Shuster**	N
NEW YORK		10 **Broyhill**	N	10 McDade	Y
1 **Carney**	Y	11 Gudger	N	11 Flood	?
2 Downey	Y	**NORTH DAKOTA**		12 Murtha	Y
3 Ambro	Y	1 **Andrews**	?	13 **Coughlin**	Y
4 **Lent**	Y	**OHIO**		14 Moorhead	Y
5 **Wydler**	N	1 **Gradison**	C	15 **Ritter**	N
6 Wolff	—	2 Luken	Y	16 **Walker**	N
7 Addabbo	Y	3 Hall	Y	17 Ertel	Y
8 Rosenthal	Y	4 **Guyer**	Y	18 Walgren	Y
9 Ferraro	Y	5 **Latta**	Y	19 **Goodling**	Y
10 Biaggi	Y	6 **Harsha**	Y	20 Gaydos	Y
11 Scheuer	Y	7 **Brown**	N	21 Bailey	Y
12 Chisholm	Y	8 **Kindness**	N	22 Murphy	Y
13 Solarz	Y	9 Ashley	Y	23 **Clinger**	N
14 Richmond	?	10 **Miller**	N	24 Marks	Y
15 Zeferetti	Y	11 **Stanton**	N	25 Atkinson	Y
16 Holtzman	Y	12 **Devine**	N		

RHODE ISLAND
1 St. Germain — Y
2 Beard — N
SOUTH CAROLINA
1 Davis — Y
2 **Spence** — Y
3 **Derrick** — Y
4 **Campbell** — N
5 Holland — Y
6 Jenrette — Y
SOUTH DAKOTA
1 Daschle — Y
2 **Abdnor** — N
TENNESSEE
1 **Quillen** — Y
2 **Duncan** — Y
3 Bouquard — Y
4 Gore — Y
5 Baner — Y
6 **Beard** — N
7 Jones — Y
8 Ford — Y
TEXAS
1 Hall — Y
2 Wilson, C. — Y
3 **Collins** — N
4 Roberts — Y
5 Mattox — Y
6 Gramm — N
7 **Archer** — N

8 Eckhardt — Y
9 Brooks — ?
10 Pickle — Y
11 Leath — Y
12 Wright — Y
13 Hightower — Y
14 Wyatt — Y
15 de la Garza — N
16 White — N
17 Stenholm — Y
18 Leland — Y
19 Hance — Y
20 Gonzalez — Y
21 **Loeffler** — X
22 **Paul** — N
23 Kazen — Y
24 Frost — Y
UTAH
1 McKay — Y
2 **Marriott** — Y
VERMONT
1 **Jeffords** — N
VIRGINIA
1 **Trible** — N
2 **Whitehurst** — Y
3 Satterfield — N
4 **Daniel, R.W.** — N
5 Daniel, D. — N
6 **Butler** — N

7 **Robinson** — N
8 Harris — N
9 **Wampler** — Y
10 Fisher — N
WASHINGTON
1 **Pritchard** — N
2 Swift — N
3 Bonker — Y
4 McCormack — Y
5 Foley — Y
6 Dicks — Y
7 Lowry — N
WEST VIRGINIA
1 Mollohan — Y
2 Staggers — Y
3 Slack — Y
4 Rahall — Y
WISCONSIN
1 Aspin — Y
2 Kastenmeier — Y
3 Baldus — Y
4 Zablocki — Y
5 Reuss — Y
6 Petri — N
7 Obey — Y
8 **Roth** — N
9 **Sensenbrenner** — N
WYOMING
1 **Cheney** — N

Senate Vote

ALABAMA
Heflin — Y
Stewart — Y
ALASKA
Gravel — N
Stevens — Y
ARIZONA
DeCancini — N
Goldwater — -
ARKANSAS
Bumpers — N
Pryor — N
CALIFORNIA
Cranston — Y
Hayakawa — N
COLORADO
Hart — N
Armstrong — N
CONNECTICUT
Ribicoff — N
Weicker — N
DELAWARE
Biden — Y
Roth — Y
FLORIDA
Chiles — Y
Stone — Y
GEORGIA
Nunn — N
Talmadge — Y
HAWAII
Inouye — Y

Matsunaga — Y
IDAHO
Church — Y
McClure — N
ILLINOIS
Stevenson — N
Percy — Y
INDIANA
Bayh — Y
Lugar — Y
IOWA
Culver — Y
Jepsen — N
KANSAS
Dole — Y
Kassebaum — N
KENTUCKY
Ford — Y
Huddleston — Y
LOUISIANA
Johnston — Y
Long — Y
MAINE
Muskie — Y
Cohen — N
MARYLAND
Sarbanes — Y
Mathias — Y
MASSACHUSETTS
Kennedy — Y
Tsongas — Y

MICHIGAN
Levin — Y
Riegle — Y
MINNESOTA
Boschwitz — N
Durenberger — N
MISSISSIPPI
Stennis — N
Cochran — N
MISSOURI
Eagleton — Y
Danforth — Y
MONTANA
Baucus — Y
Melcher — Y
NEBRASKA
Exon — N
Zarinsky — N
NEVADA
Cannon — Y
Laxalt — N
NEW HAMPSHIRE
Durkin — Y
Humphrey — N
NEW JERSEY
Bradley — Y
Williams — Y
NEW MEXICO
Domenici — N
Schmitt — Y
NEW YORK
Moynihan — Y

Javits	Y	SOUTH CAROLINA		Magnuson	Y	
NORTH CAROLINA		Hollings	?	**WEST VIRGINIA**		
Morgan	N	**Thurmond**	N	Byrd	Y	
Helms	N	**SOUTH DAKOTA**		Randolph	Y	
NORTH DAKOTA		McGovern	Y	**WISCONSIN**		
Burdick	N	**Pressler**	N	Nelson	Y	
Young	Y	**TENNESSEE**		Proxmire	N	
OHIO		Sasser	Y	**WYOMING**		
Glenn	Y	**Baker**	?	**Simpson**	N	
Metzenbaum	Y	**TEXAS**		**Wallop**	N	
OKLAHOMA		Bentsen	Y			
Baren	N	**Tower**	Y			
Bellman	N	**UTAH**				
OREGON		**Garn**	N			
Hatfield	N	**Hatch**	N			
Packwood	N	**VERMONT**				
PENNSYLVANIA		Leahy	Y			
Heinz	N	**Stafford**	Y			
Schweiker	N	**VIRGINIA**				
RHODE ISLAND		Byrd	N			
Pell	N	**Warner**	N			
Chafee	N	**WASHINGTON**				
SOUTH CAROLINA		Jackson	Y			

Acknowledgments

Spring 1974, A.M. Rosenthal, then the managing editor of *The New York Times,* asked a prospective reporter for the newspaper to put aside an insatiable desire to continue writing about public education and politics in the South and focus that energy on the world of business.

A reluctant, yet affirmative response to the request from Rosenthal, now the executive editor of the *Times,* formed the foundation of my business writing career, subsequently nursed by Thomas Mullaney, Richard Mooney, John Lee and David R. Jones, national editor of the *Times* and former chief of the Detroit bureau. To each of these fellow journalists and to Condon Rodgers, one of the best copy editors on the *Times* staff, my special thanks for your support over the years.

Robert Lindsey, chief of *The New York Times* Los Angeles bureau, and John Egerton, Nashville-based freelance writer are due many thanks for encouraging me to pursue book writing as a vehicle for expanded communications, despite its frustration. Robert Irvin and Jerry Flint, two seasoned automotive writers whose knowledge could comprise several volumes of never-a-dull-moment reading, should be credited with helping me learn the ropes of the industry and dissect its jargon.

And to Jeanne Fox, who labored through many days and nights as manuscript editor of this book, my thanks a million times over. Likewise, my hat goes off to Janet A. Murray, a laid-off Chrysler worker who fought the unemployment-line blues while serving as manuscript typist.

Without the cooperation of dozens of present and former employees of The Chrysler Corporation and its competitors, this book could not have been successfully completed. Their working knowledge of the company and industry, often shared reluctantly, provided the invaluable insight needed to breathe life into the numbers that dominate this business and helped me to sort out the crucial developments from those not so important. I would like to thank many of them publicly, particularly those who tolerated midnight interviews in order to help speed the research and preparation of this book. But their wishes to remain anonymous will be respected.

Help in selected research areas was rendered by Eileen Sullivan of the Detroit Public Library, Al Rothenberg of the Motor Vehicle Manufacturers Association, the Photography Staff and Library Staff of the *Detroit Free Press*, Zachare Ball of the *Free Press,* and Joyce Esbin of *The Los Angeles Times.*

In Washington and New York, a special thanks to the dozens of government and financial community workers who offered their views and insight into how Detroit functions and why various automobile makers made the decisions they made and took the actions that they did.

To the staff of *and books,* my thanks for your tireless efforts in expediting the publication of this work at a time when Americans could stand to know more than one is able to tell in a matter of minutes with a microphone, tape recorder and pictures or a few paragraphs.

Excellent. You have all been excellent. I hope this work is one of which we can all be proud.

Reginald Stuart

Index